Complexity and the Experience of Values, Conflict and Compromise in Organizations

What role do values play in organizational life? How do they shape the efficiency and effectiveness of organizational change? This volume examines what we actually mean when we use the term values and what it means to act according to values in ordinary everyday life. The contributors to this volume provide an exposition of the circular relationship between values, conflict, and compromise.

It can be said that current research lacks a thorough exploration of what we actually mean by human values and what it means to act according to values in ordinary, everyday life in organizations. This is what the chapters in this volume seek to address through the reflections of organizational practitioners on their ordinary work in organizations. Such reflection reveals that values are indeed important in the motivation to act in organizational life but that they cannot be "used" in the instrumental manner suggested by mainstream literature and they certainly do not lead to harmony. Indeed, the essence of acting according to value commitments is found to be conflict and the question raised is how people negotiate this conflict in their everyday organizational lives. The contributors examine how such negotiation brings with it the need to compromise. However, on other occasions a "no compromise" response seems to be called for, and when and how such a response is to be made depends upon one's values. The chapters in this volume seek to raise awareness of the issues involved in this endlessly circular relationship between values, conflict, and compromise.

Covering subject areas such as organizational theory and behavior, and organizational analysis as well as the sociology of work and industry, this book will appeal to researchers and practitioners alike.

Ralph Stacey is Director and Professor of Management at the Complexity and Management Centre, University of Hertfordshire, UK. **Douglas Griffin** is Visiting Professor and Assistant Director at the Complexity and Management Centre, University of Hertfordshire, UK.

Routledge studies in complexity in management

Complexity and the Experience of Values, Conflict and Compromise in Organizations

Edited by Ralph Stacey and Douglas Griffin

Routledge
Taylor & Francis Group

LONDON AND NEW YORK

First published 2008
by Routledge
2 Park Square, Milton Park, Abingdon, Oxon OX14 4RN

Simultaneously published in the USA and Canada
by Routledge
270 Madison Ave, New York, NY 10016

Routledge is an imprint of the Taylor & Francis Group, an informa business

Typeset in Times by Wearset Ltd, Boldon, Tyne and Wear
Printed and bound in Great Britain by TJI Digital, Padstow, Cornwall

British Library Cataloguing in Publication Data
A catalogue record for this book is available from the British Library

Library of Congress Cataloging in Publication Data
Complexity and the experience of values, conflict, and compromise in
organizations/edited by Ralph Stacey and Douglas Griffin.
p. cm.
Includes bibliographical references and index.
1. Organizational effectiveness. 2. Complex organizations–Management.
3. Interorganizational relations. 4. Organizational change. 5. Corporate
culture. I. Stacey, Ralph D. II. Griffin, Douglas, 1946–

HD58.9.C647 2008
658.4'01–dc22

                                                                2007043219

ISBN10: 0-415-45726-2 (hbk)
ISBN10: 0-203-92812-1 (ebk)

ISBN13: 978-0-415-45726-2 (hbk)
ISBN13: 978-0-415-92812-7 (ebk)

Contents

vi   *Contents*

Contributors

Stephen Billing is an independent consultant in New Zealand and is completing his Doctor of Management thesis at the University of Hertfordshire.

Martin Daly is a Catholic priest and headmaster of a large school in Dublin. He is completing his Doctor of Management thesis at the University of Hertfordshire.

Iver Drabæk is an independent consultant in Denmark and is completing his Doctor of Management thesis at the University of Hertfordshire.

Douglas Griffin is an independent consultant, visiting Professor at the Business School of the University of Hertfordshire and Associate Director of the Complexity and Management Centre.

Arnie Grant is the managing director of a division of a large services company. He is completing his Doctor of Management thesis at the University of Hertfordshire.

Chris Mowles is an independent consultant in the UK and has completed his Doctor of Management thesis at the University of Hertfordshire.

Ralph Stacey is Professor of Management at the Business School of the University of Hertfordshire and Director of its Complexity and Management Centre. He is also a member of the Institute of Group Analysis.

1 Introduction

Ralph Stacey and Douglas Griffin

The most prevalent ways of making sense of intricate and confusing organizational situations concentrate mainly on the rational and predictable aspects of human experience, leading to attempts at programmatic, large-scale management of change applied to the organization which is understood as a system. However, there is some research evidence that most of the large scale change programs do not achieve the successful outcomes, financial and otherwise, anticipated at their outset. Such lack of success is usually attributed to failure to take sufficient account of the "human factor". Despite these findings most managers and many researchers continue to focus on the same rational, large scale change programs, adding large scale motivational and culture change programs to hopefully take more account of the "human factor". The lack of success, however, continues. We hold that what is called for in this situation is a radical re-examination of currently dominant ways of making sense of organizational life, one which questions the foundational assumption that organizations can be understood as systems.

Members of the Complexity and Management Centre at the Business School of the University of Hertfordshire have been developing an alternative perspective according to which organizations are understood as population-wide patterns of relating which emerge in *complex responsive processes* of daily local interaction between people. The focus of attention here is on how wide-spread change emerges as people interact locally in everyday situations. Organizations are understood to be ongoing, iterated processes of cooperative and competitive relating between people. They are not systems but rather the ongoing patterning of interactions between people. Patterns of human interaction produce further patterns of interaction, not some *thing* outside of the interaction. We called this perspective the theory of *complex responsive processes of relating*. This theory draws on analogies from the complexity sciences, bringing in the essential characteristics of human agents, namely consciousness and self consciousness, understood to emerge in social processes of communicative interaction, power relating and evaluative choice. The result is a way of thinking about life in organizations that focuses attention on how organizational members cope with the *unknown* as they perpetually create organizational futures together. The theory of complex responsive processes was initially developed in a series of books called *Complexity and Emergence in Organizations* edited by some members of the Complexity and Management Centre (Stacey *et al.*, 2000; Stacey, 2001; Streatfield, 2001; Fonseca, 2001; Griffin, 2002; Shaw, 2002) (see also Stacey, 2007).

Since 2000, some of the authors in the series, together with other Complexity and Management Centre colleagues have been conducting a research degree program on organizational change leading to the degrees of Master of Arts by research or Doctor of Management. The program is for experienced leaders and managers, as well as internal and external consultants, who are interested in questioning, reflecting upon and developing the effectiveness of their current work, particularly how they think about what they are doing. The theory of complex responsive processes provides a provocative perspective for stimulating participants' reflections. This is necessarily a part time program because the core of the research method (Stacey and Griffin, 2005) involves students taking their own experience seriously. If patterns of human interaction produce nothing but further patterns of human interaction, in the creation of which we are all partici- pating, then there is no *detached* way of understanding organizations from the position of the objective observer. Instead, organizations have to be understood in terms of one's own personal experience of participating with others in the co- creation of the patterns of interaction that are the organization. The students' research is, therefore, their narration of current events they are *involved* in together with their reflections on themes of particular importance emerging in the stories of their own experience of participation with others. The research stance is, then, one of detached involvement and it is essentially reflexive in that it requires "locating" one's thinking not only in relation to one's own life experience but importantly in relation to the history and current context of one's society, especially the history of its thought as expressed in relevant literature. This kind of "location" helps one to identify the assumptions upon which a particular way of thinking is built.

The Doctor of Management program attracts practising leaders and managers from a range of organizations in many countries. Graduates and current particip- ants come from the USA, Canada, Norway, Denmark, Finland, Germany, Netherlands, Israel, New Zealand, South Africa, Ireland and the UK and they work in public and private sector organizations as well as nonprofit organi- zations. They are employees of public and private sector organizations and are also self employed consultants to organizations. A number of them are Chief Executives, directors and university professors. The research community of the program is therefore well placed to generate material and insight into the daily practices of actual organizational life and it is building up a body of knowledge about what managers and leaders actually do at the micro level. Some of this research has been published in a series of edited volumes called *Complexity and Emergence in Organizations*, published in London by Routledge. The books in the series are addressed to organizational practitioners and academics who are looking for a different way of making sense of their own experience in a rapidly changing world and present reflective accounts of ordinary everyday life in organizations, rather than idealized accounts or further idealized prescriptions. There are five volumes in this series (Stacey and Griffin, 2005, 2006; Griffin and Stacey, 2005; Stacey, 2005; Shaw and Stacey, 2006).

This volume has the same purpose as those in the above series, and like the volumes in that series its contributors are members of the Doctor of Management program. It focuses attention on an issue which for some years now has attracted the attention of a great many leaders and managers in organizations of all kinds, ranging from major international banks, oil companies, public sector services and international nongovernmental organizations to small local charities. That issue has to do with the role that values play in organizational life generally and in the quality, efficiency and effectiveness of organizational change and improvement. There has been a growing awareness of the powerful motivating effects of the values people are inspired by and the importance of the self control which belief in values instills. This interest has been most visibly expressed in various prescriptions for designing values, usually seen as the role of leaders, and converting organizational members to believe in, and act upon, the shared values expressed in value statements, missions and visions. The result of this effort has been highly generalized and idealized propositional statements, which are supposed to lead to unquestioning harmony but instead often provoke cynicism on the part of organizational members, with little evidence that it all achieves much. What is lacking is exploration of what we actually mean by human values and what it means to act according to values in ordinary, everyday life in organizations. This is what the chapters in this volume seek to address through the reflections of organizational practitioners on their ordinary work in organizations.

Such reflection reveals that values are indeed important in the motivation to act in organizational life but that they cannot be "used" in the instrumental manner suggested by mainstream literature and they certainly do not lead simply to harmony. Indeed, the essence of acting according to value commitments is inevitably conflict. Values are idealizations which necessarily have to be interpreted in contingent situations and this inevitably leads to conflict. The question becomes how people negotiate this conflict in their ordinary everyday organizational lives. Such negotiation brings with it the need to compromise. However, on other occasions a "no compromise" response seems to be called for, and when and how such a response is to be made depends upon one's values. The chapters in this volume seek to raise awareness of the issues involved in this endlessly circular relationship between values, conflict and compromise. The aim is to contribute to a more robust articulation of these issues in organizations.

This chapter provides a brief summary of the theory of complex responsive processes since all the chapters in this volume make reference to it and further develop it in a number of ways. This chapter concludes with short summaries of the chapters in the rest of the book.

The theory of complex responsive processes

The theory of complex responsive processes is a theory of human action which draws on analogies from the complexity sciences, particularly the theory of complex adaptive systems.

Complex adaptive systems consist of large numbers of agents, each of which interacts with some other agents. The interaction between the agents can thus be said to be local in that each agent is interacting, according to their own rules of interaction, with only a small proportion of the total population of agents. In other words, each agent is a set of rules specifying how it must interact with others and the interaction between agents is self organizing in that the agents are not being instructed by any other agent – each is following its own instructions – not any centrally determined rules. This does not amount to anarchy because each agent cannot do whatever it likes – it must follow its rules of interaction and cannot do other than this. In this way each agent constrains and is constrained by other agents and these constraints often conflict with each other. The properties of complex adaptive systems are explored through computer simulations (for example, Kauffman, 1995; Ray, 1992) in which each agent is a computer program, a set of rules (digital symbols) specifying interaction with some other agents. The simulation is the iterative interaction of these agents. Large numbers of such simulations repeatedly demonstrate that such iterative, local interaction produces global patterns of order or coherence, which emerge, paradoxically predictable and unpredictable at the same time, in the absence of any global program or plan. The conflicting constraints that the agents place on each other are essential to this emergent order. Furthermore, when these agents are different to each other, then both they and the global patterns emerging in their interaction evolve, so producing novelty (Allen, 1998a, 1998b).

Instead of thinking that local interaction is producing a global whole, or system, we could think of patterns of local interaction as producing further patterns of both local interaction and global patterns at the same time. There is then no need to think in terms of systems or wholes. Global patterns are changing not because of some global plan but because of local interaction. If this were to apply to human interaction it would indicate a rather profound shift in how we think about organizations. We usually think that global organizational order is the result of global plans and programs but from the perspective just outlined we would have to think of global organizational order as continually emerging in myriad local interactions and it would become necessary to understand the nature of such local interaction. Is there any basis for such a shift in thinking?

The simulations just referred to are highly abstract, showing the properties of certain kinds of abstract interaction between abstract agents in the domain of digital symbols. To be useful in any other domain, say biology, it is necessary to bring to these abstract relationships the attributes of that particular domain. In other words, the simulations can only ever be a source domain for analogies that might be useful in some other domain when interpreted in terms of the attributes of that other domain. In thinking about the implications of complex adaptive system simulations for human action it is essential, therefore, to take account of the nature of human agents. First, it is highly simplistic to think of humans as rule following beings. In our acting, we may take account of rules but can hardly be said to blindly follow them as the digital agents in computer simulations do. The essential and distinctive characteristic of human agents is that they are living bodies who are conscious and self conscious beings capable of emotion, spontaneity, improvisation, imagination, fantasy and creative action. Human agents are essentially reflexive and reflective. Furthermore, they are essentially social beings in a distinctive way in that they do not interact blindly according to mechanistic rules but engage in meaningful communicative interaction with each other in which they establish power relations between themselves. In addition, in interacting with each other humans exercise at least some degree of choice as to how they will respond to the actions of others and this involves the use of some form of evaluative criteria. In addition, human agents use both simple and more and more complicated tools and technologies to accomplish what they choose to do. It is these embodied attributes of consciousness, self consciousness, reflection and reflexivity, creativity, imagination and fantasy, communication, meaning, power, choice, evaluation, tool use and sociality that should be explicitly brought to any interpretation, as regards human beings, of the insights derived from complex adaptive system simulations.

As soon as one does explicitly take account of the above essential attributes of human agents then it becomes problematic to talk about human systems. Some 250 years ago, Kant introduced the notion of system as a useful way of understanding organisms in nature but cautioned against applying this notion to human action. A system is a whole produced by its parts and separated by a boundary from other wholes. A part is only a part insofar as it is doing what is required to produce the whole. If one thought of a human individual as a part then by definition that individual could not exercise his or her own local choices. If individuals did make their own choices then they could not be said to be parts of a system because they would be acting in their own interests instead of in the interest of the system. In addition to making choices, humans form figurations of power relations in which they act in the interests of their own group, often in conflict with other groups. They are then not acting in the interest of a wider, more global system, but in their own joint interests. Human agents cannot, therefore, be thought of as parts of a system because individually and collectively they exercise choices and engage in power plays. If one is to think of humans designing a system then one encounters the problem that the designer has to be thought of as taking an observer position outside the system in order to design it. But the designer, being human, is also part of the system. Second order systems thinking (for example, Jackson, 2000; Midgley, 2000) tries to address this problem by widening the boundary of the system to include the observer. But this simply sets up the need for an outside observer of the wider system so leading to an argument characterized by infinite regress.

Furthermore, with one exception, systems models cannot explain how anything novel could arise because a system is always unfolding the pattern already enfolded in it by its rules of operation. The one exception is complex adaptive systems consisting of agents characterized by diversity. Here, the model takes on a life of its own, as it were, evolving unpredictably in ways that no one has programed. This is the same as saying that of its very essence no one can design its evolution as small differences are amplified into significant, unforeseeable changes. The agents in such a system are forming the system while being formed by it at the same time but in a mechanistic way in which they display no consciousness, self consciousness, imagination, reflexivity, choice, creativity or spontaneity. Furthermore, there are practical problems with such a system model. If the model takes on a life of its own, while the phenomenon being modeled also takes on a life of its own, then it is highly unlikely that both will follow the same trajectory. The explanatory power of the model is then questionable. It also becomes unclear what might be meant by a "boundary" or a "whole" in relation to such a system model. If it is evolving in unpredictable ways, the "whole" will always be incomplete and the boundary unclear. It seems to us that in pointing to the nature of their dynamics, heterogeneous complex adaptive system models begin to unravel the usefulness of thinking in systems terms at all when it comes to human action.

What then is an alternative way of thinking about the relationship between local interaction and global pattern, one that takes explicit account of the central features of human agency listed above? The alternative is to take as analogies the properties of iterative interaction, or temporal process, from the domain of heterogeneous complex adaptive systems and interpret them in terms of key human attributes. It is this approach that leads to the theory of complex responsive processes.

Organizations understood as complex responsive processes of relating

A key property of complex adaptive systems, referred to above, is that of processes of interaction in digital symbols patterning themselves as both local and global order at the same time. How might we take this abstract relationship from the domain of complex adaptive systems to the domain of human interaction? Well, human interaction is basically responsive communication between human bodies where each is conscious and self conscious, and so capable of reflection, reflexivity, imagination and fantasy, thereby having some choice and displaying some spontaneity. To signal the move from the domain of computer simulations and systems to that of the temporal processes of human interaction we refer to complex responsive processes instead of complex adaptive systems. The first key aspect of the complex responsive process of relating between human bodies is communicative interaction and George Herbert Mead's (1934) theories of conversation provide a powerful way of understanding this. It leads us to think of organizations as ongoing temporal processes of human communicative interaction.

Communicative interaction

Drawing on the work of the American pragmatist, George Herbert Mead, one can understand consciousness as arising in the communicative interaction between human bodies. Humans have evolved central nervous systems such that when one gestures to another, particularly in the form of vocal gesture or language, one evokes in one's own body responses to one's gesture that are similar to those evoked in other bodies. Mead refers to this as communication in the medium of significant symbols. In other words, in their acting, humans take the attitude, the tendency to act, of the other and it is because they have this capacity to communicate in significant symbols that humans can know what they are doing. It immediately follows that consciousness (knowing, mind) is a social process in which meaning emerges in the social act of gesture-response, where the gesture can never be separated from the response. Meaning does not lie in the gesture, the word, alone but only in the gesture taken together with the response to it. Human communicative interaction is then understood as an iterative, ongoing process in which a gesture by one, which is itself a response to a previous gesture, evokes responses in others. In this ongoing responding to each other, each is simultaneously intending a gesture and having it evoked by others. In a lifetime of interaction people develop expectations of how others will respond to them as they try to fit in with, or diverge from, each other in their ordinary, everyday activities. Since each has the capacity for spontaneity, for surprising even themselves, no one can control or be totally sure of the responses of others and thus of the meaning which will emerge in their interactions. Human communicative interaction is thus essentially predicable and unpredictable at the same time and so involves taking risks of being misunderstood and experiencing the anxiety this brings. It is these aspects of spontaneity, simultaneous predictability and unpredictability, risk taking and its potential for anxiety that are so characteristic of improvisational action. This is the theoretical foundation for the emphasis on the improvisational nature of activity in organizations.

Furthermore, in communicating with each other, as the basis of everything they do, people do not simply take the attitude of the specific others with whom they are relating at any one time. Humans have the capacity for generalizing so that when they act they always take up the attitude of what Mead called the generalized other. In other words, they always take the attitude of the group or society to their actions – they are concerned about what others might think of what they do or say. This is often unconscious and it is, of course, a powerful form of social control.

Human society is a society of selves and selves exist only in relation to other selves. A self is an individual who organizes his or her own response by the tendencies on the part of others to respond to his or her act. Self exists in taking the role of others. According to Mead, self-consciousness is thus a social process involving the capacity humans have as subjects to take themselves as an object. This is a social process because the subject, "I", can only ever be an object to itself as "me" and the "me" is one's perception of the attitude of society toward oneself. The "I" is the often spontaneous and imaginative response of the socially formed individual to the "me" as the gesture of society to oneself. Self is thus temporal processes, an "I-me" dialectic, where "I" and "me" are inseparable phases of the same action, so that each self is socially formed while at the same time interacting selves are forming the social. Communication, then, is not simply the sending of a signal to be received by another, but rather complex social, that is, responsive, processes of self formation in which meaning and society-wide patterns emerge. One cannot, therefore, be a self independently of social interaction. Selves are social selves and society is a society of selves.

For Mead, mind is a private role play/silent conversation of a body with itself and the social is the public, vocal interaction or conversation between bodies. Furthermore, such gestures indicate to others how the social act is likely to unfold further. Mead explains what he means by an individual calling forth a similar response in herself as in the other. He means that she is taking the attitude of the other and he defines attitude as the tendency to act in a particular way. Mind then is the activity of experiencing a similar attitude, a similar tendency to act in a particular way, in response to gestures directed to others. Mind here is clearly a social phenomenon. In Mead's work we have a theory of consciousness and self consciousness emerging in the social interaction between human bodies in the medium of significant symbols and at the same time widespread social patterns also emerge. Human interaction forms and is formed by the social at the same time.

Particularly important in this way of understanding human interaction is the human capacity for generalizing, for taking the attitude of the generalized other as consciousness and the "me" phase of the "I-me" dialectic where the "me" is the generalized attitude of the society to the "I". Mead's main concern was not simply with a dyadic form of communication but with much wider, much more complex patterns of interaction between many people. He was concerned with complex social acts in which many people are engaged in conversations through which they accomplish the tasks of fitting in and conflicting with each other to realize their objectives and purposes. People do not come to an interaction with each other afresh each time because they are born into an already existing, socially evolved pattern and they continue to play their part in its further evolution. This leads Mead to his concept of the generalized other. In order to accomplish complex social acts, it is not enough for those involved to be able to take the attitude of the small numbers of people they may be directly engaged with at a particular time. They need to be able to take the attitude of all of those directly or indirectly engaged in the complex social act. It would be impossible to do this in relation to each individual so engaged but humans have developed the capacity to generalize the attitudes of many. In acting in the present, each individual is then taking up the attitude of a few specific others and at the same time the attitude of this generalized other, the attitude of the group, the organization or the society. These wider, generalized attitudes are evolving historically and are always implicated in every human action. In play, the child takes the role of another. But in the game the child must take on not only the role of the other but of the game, that is, of all participants in the game and its rules and procedures. The generalized other is the taking of the attitude of all other participants.

In the evolution of society many generalizations emerge which are taken up, or particularized in people's interactions with each other. This is a point of major importance. Mead draws attention to paradoxical processes of generalization and particularization at the same time. Mental and social activities are processes of generalizing and particularizing at the same time. Individuals act in relation to that which is common to all of them (generalizing) but responded to somewhat differently by each of them in each present time period (particularizing).

Mead provided a number of formulations of these generalizing-particularizing processes. One such formulation is his explanation of self consciousness referred to above. In understanding self consciousness Mead talked about a person taking the attitude of the group to himself, where that attitude is the "me". It is important to bear in mind that Mead was saying something more than that the self arises in the attitude, the tendency to act, of specific others toward oneself. Mead was talking about a social, generalizing process where the "me" is a generalization across a whole community or society. For example what it means to be an individual, a person, a man or a woman, a professional, and so on, does not arise in relation to a few specific people but in relation to a particular society in a particular era. We in the West think of ourselves now as individuals in a completely different way to people in the West did 400 years ago and a different way to people in other cultures. In the "I-me" dialectic, then, we have a process in which the generalization of the "me" is made particular in the response of the "I" for a particular person at a particular time in a particular place. For example, one may take up what it means to be a man in society in a particular way that differs in some respects to how others see themselves as men in our own society, in other societies and at other times.

Mead's discussion of what he called the social object is yet another formulation of this generalizing and particularizing process. Mead distinguishes between a physical object and a social object. A physical object exists in nature and is the proper object of study in the natural sciences, while the social object is the proper object of study in the social sciences. While the physical object can be understood in terms of itself, the social object has to be understood in terms of social acts. Mead referred to market exchange as an example of a social act. When one person offers to buy food this act obviously involves a complex range of responses from other people to provide the food. However, it involves more than this because the one making the offer can only know how to make the offer if he is able to take the attitude of the other parties to the bargain. All essential phases of the complex social act of exchange must appear in the actions of all involved and appear as essential features of each individual's actions. Buying and selling are involved in each other.

Mead, therefore, defined the social act as one involving the cooperation of many people in which the different parts of the act undertaken by different individuals appear in the act of each individual. The tendencies to act as others act are present in the conduct of each individual involved and it is this presence that is responsible for the appearance of the social object in the experience of each individual. The social act defines the object of the act and this is a social object which is only to be found in the conduct of the different individuals engaged in the complex social act. The social object appears in the experience of each individual as a stimulus to a response not only by that individual but also by the others involved – this is how each can know how the others are likely to act and it is the basis of coordination. A social object is thus a kind of gesture together with tendencies to respond in particular ways. Social objects are common plans or patterns of action related to the existent future of the act. The social object is a generalization which is taken up, or particularized, by all in a group/society in their actions. Social objects have evolved in the history of the society of selves and each individual is born into such a world of social objects. The conduct of individuals marks out and defines the social objects which make up their environment, in which the nature of the social objects and the sensitivities of individuals answer to each other. In other words, individuals are forming social objects while being formed by them in an evolutionary process.

Mead linked social objects to social control. Social control is the bringing of the act of the individual into relation with the social object, and the contours of the object determine the organization of the act. The social act is distributed amongst many but the whole social object appears in the experience of all of them. Social control depends upon the degree to which the individual takes the attitude of the others, that is, takes the attitude which is the social object. All institutions are social objects and serve to control individuals who find them in their experience.

It is important to note here how the generalizations, the social objects referred to above, are only to be found in the way in which they are being made particular at any one time in any one contingent situation. People are continually interpreting and negotiating with each other the meaning of the generalizations that have emerged and continue to evolve in the myriad ongoing local interactions between people. This continual interpretation and negotiation in local situations involves responsiveness, imagination, spontaneity and all the other aspects of improvisational activity so providing a complex, richer theoretical foundation for the arguments developed in this book.

Mead also linked social objects to values and in another formulation of the interaction between the general and the particular, he draws a distinction between cult values and their functionalization. Cult values are idealizations that emerge in the evolution of a society. Mead said that they were the most precious part of our heritage and examples of cult values are democracy, treating others with respect, regarding life as sacred, belief in being American or British, and so on. Other examples are mission and vision statements in organizations. Such cult values present people with the image of an idealized future shorn of all constraints. If such values are applied directly to action, without allowing for variations contingent on a specific situation, then those undertaking such action form a cult in which they exclude all who do not comply. In the usual course of events, however, this does not happen as people act on present interpretations of cult values. For example, a cult value to do with the sacredness of life is not directly applied in some places leading to conflict regarding, for example, abortion. Functionalization of cult values inevitably leads to conflict and the negotiation of compromises around such conflict. Functionalizing of values is the enactment of values in the ordinary, local interactions between people in the living present. In his notion of cult values, Mead points not only to the generalizing tendencies of interacting people but also to the idealizing tendencies characteristic of their interaction. Such idealizations may be good or bad depending upon who is doing the judging. Mead's notions of social objects and cult values have something in common with the notions of social structure, habit and routine. What was distinctive about Mead's approach to these matters, however, is how he avoided positing social structure as a phenomenon that exists outside individuals. Social objects and cult values are generalizations and idealizations that only have any existence in their particularization in the ordinary, everyday interactions between people in the living present. What happens as people try to functionalize cult values are processes of interpretation and negotiation which always carry the potential for spontaneity, the properties of predictability and unpredictability characteristic of improvisational activity. Once again Mead's perspective on values provides a theoretical foundation for taking an improvisational approach to understanding life in organizations.

The second key aspect of complex responsive processes of relating has to do with power. Here the work of Norbert Elias is particularly instructive.

Relations of power

Drawing on the work of Elias (1939), one understands how the processes of communicative interacting constitute relations of power. For Elias, power is not something anyone possesses but, rather, is a characteristic of all human relating. In order to form, and stay in, a relationship with someone else, one cannot do whatever one wants. As soon as we enter into relationships, therefore, we constrain and are constrained by others and, of course, we also enable and are enabled by others. There is a clear analogy with the conflicting constraints characteristic of the complex adaptive system simulations described earlier in this chapter. In human action, power is this enabling-constraining relationship where the power balance is tilted in favor of some and against others depending on the relative need they have for each other, for example, one may have control over resources that others need. Elias showed how such power relationships form figurations, or groupings, in which some are included and others are excluded and where the power balance is tilted in favor of some groupings and against others. These groupings establish powerful feelings of belonging which constitute each individual's "we" identity. These "we" identities, derived from the groups we belong to, are inseparable from each of our "I" identities. As with Mead, then, we can see that processes of human relating form and are formed by individual and collective identities, which inevitably reflect complex, conflictual and cooperative patterns of power relating. Furthermore, Elias shows how these power figurations are sustained, unconsciously, by ideologies, which are in turn sustained by gossip and processes of shame. Power relations are always made to feel natural by an unconscious underlying ideology. It is this that sustains the dominant discourse of a group which of course is reflected in patterns of power relating.

Elias' approach to power links well with Mead's notion of communicative interaction. Social object/cult value both constrain and enable mind/self and interaction (social). Another way of talking about power, then, is to talk about the enabling/constraining nature of social object and cult value as they are particularized and functionalized in local interaction in specific contingent situations. But just what form do these enabling constraints take? Some aspects are as follows:

• People form groups and they label or name such groupings. In so doing, they differentiate themselves from others in an "us" and "them" dynamic. We can, therefore, describe processes of power, of enabling and constraining, in terms of the dynamics of inclusion–exclusion and the formation of identity in local interaction in contingent situations.

• Enabling and constraining can also be understood as activities of cooperating and competing and this immediately directs attention to the motivations of altruism and self centeredness or rivalry, driven by the desire to retain and strengthen identity and belonging. The rivalry is frequently around which discourse is to dominate and about control of resources too.

• The emotions of shame, envy and jealousy as well as empathy, compassion and acceptance also help to explain the manner in which people constrain and enable each other.

• Fantasy and imagination as well as acting and thinking in defensive ways (social and individual) are also ways of describing the enabling and constraining activities of relating.

• We can describe enabling and constraining activities in terms of politics and negotiation processes and the often conflicting ideologies underlying these processes.

• Throughout we are talking about cooperation and conflict and how they are dealt with. For Mead conflict is intrinsic to particularizing, functionalizing processes.

When we talk about complex responsive processes of relating, therefore, we are talking about the complex emotions and motivations, as well as the spontaneity and imagination which characterize ordinary, everyday communicating and power relating in organizations. What we have been describing is the complex, improvisational nature of human relating, so pointing to the theoretical basis for claiming that organizational life is improvisational.

Choices arising in acts of evaluation

In their communicative interacting and power relating, humans are always making choices between one action and another. This may be on the basis of conscious desires and intentions, or unconscious desires and choices, for example, those that are habitual, impulsive, obsessive or compulsive. In other words, human action is always evaluative, sometimes consciously and at other times unconsciously. The criteria for evaluating these choices are values and norms, together constituting ideology. This aspect is explored more fully in Chapter 2 in Griffin and Stacey, 2005.

Norms (morals, the right, the "ought") are evaluative criteria taking the form of obligatory restrictions which have emerged as generalizations and become habitual in a history of social interaction (Joas, 2000). We are all socialized to take up the norms of the particular groups and the society to which we belong and this restricts what we can do as we particularize the generalized norms in our moment by moment specific action situations. Elias' work shows in detail how norms constitute major aspects of the personality structures, or identities, of interdependent people. *Values* (ethics, the "good") are individually felt voluntary compulsions to choose one desire, action, or norm rather than another. Values arise in social processes of self formation and self transcendence (Joas, 2000; Dewey, 1934) – they are fundamental aspects of self, giving meaning to life, opening up opportunities for action. They arise in intense interactive experiences which are seized by the imagination and idealized as some "whole" to which people then feel strongly committed. Mead (1923) described these as cult values, which need to be functionalized in particular contingent situations and this inevitably involves conflict. Together the voluntary compulsion of values and the obligatory restriction of norms constitute *ideology*. Ideology is the basis on which people choose desires and actions and it unconsciously sustains power relations by making a particular figuration of power feel natural (Dalal, 1998). We can see, then, that complex responsive processes of human relating form, and are formed by, values, norms and ideologies as integral aspects of self/identity formation in its simultaneously individual and collective form.

Evaluative choice is another way of talking about decision making. Decision making is usually described as a step by step, linear, rational process, conducted by autonomous individuals but also sometimes in teams following clear, rational decision making procedures. Here the rational is split from the emotional, which is usually thought to interfere with rational decision making. However, recent brain research (Damasio, 1994, 1999) shows that the same areas of the brain deal with emotion and the selection of rational courses of action. Feelings and emotions act as important selectors of appropriate courses of action. Purely rational decision making is thus impossible and what we describe as rational decision making in ordinary organizational life is always embedded in feelings and emotion. We come then to understand decision making in terms of an emotional, ideological, social process of communicative interaction and power relating, rather than in terms of the thinking activity of the rational, autonomous individual. Decision making is thus characterized by the spontaneous, risk taking, anxiety provoking improvisational activity.

The thematic patterning of human experience

In the above description of the fundamental aspects of the complex responsive processes of human relating, we have referred to *patterns* of communicative interaction and *figurations* of power relations. These patterns and figurations can be understood as themes, taking both propositional and narrative forms, which emerge and re-emerge in the iteration, in each succeeding present, of the interactive processes of communication, power and evaluation. Values, norms and ideologies are examples of such themes. These themes organize the experience of being together.

Complex responsive processes of relating are, therefore, simultaneously processes of communicative interaction, power relating and ideological evaluation in which local individual selves/identities and the global patterns of the social emerge at the same time, each forming and being formed by the other at the same time. They are continually iterated as continuity and transformation which is possible because of the spontaneity of the "I" and the possibility of small differences being escalated into transformed patterns. And pattern means the largely narrative themes that are individual selves and social phenomena at the same time. And all of this can usefully be understood as improvisational activity which is certainly not haphazard, impulsive or thoughtless activity but highly complex, skilled performances of interdependent people.

But how does strategy and planning feature in this account?

In the literature on organizations, and in the way managers in organizations talk, strategic planning means deciding on some kind of global outcome for some long term period, say five years. This is thought first and action later, thought before action. The plan or design is the "thought" and the implementation is the "action". The assumption then is that it is possible to design global patterns well before they are realized and this in turn implies that it is possible to predict the outcomes of action to a useful degree. Local interaction is then understood as the process of implementing the plan or design. This is the essence of the planning and design schools of strategic management in the literature, it is how managers think and talk in business organizations, and it is what governments have imported from business as the basis of centralized, managerialist forms of public sector governance (Stacey and Griffin, 2005). A number of writers and practitioners have been critical of this approach for some time, a prominent writer being Mintzberg (Mintzberg *et al.*, 1998). Mintzberg and others favor another school of strategy in which organizations learn their way into the future and they distinguish between deliberate and emergent strategy. The emphasis shifts from planning to processes of learning. Senge (1990) is a key writer here and he identifies five disciplines of the learning organization: systems thinking, mental models, visions, personal mastery, and team working. He claims that organizations develop according to a limited number of general archetypes and that systems thinking allows managers to identify leverage points in organizations and then operate on them to shift from a dysfunctional archetype. So here too we get the idea that global patterns can be identified beforehand and changed directly through operating at leverage points. Local interaction then becomes working in teams to learn and so shift individual mental models and global archetypes. In both cases the focus of attention is on the global and long term and it is thought possible to operate directly on the global in some way so as to actualize prior intention regarding the global.

A complex responsive processes perspective emphasizes the unpredictability of long term outcomes/patterns, holding that design and planning with regard to the global can only achieve what it claims to achieve with regard to short term, repetitive and thus reasonably predictable activity. Even then any plans, designs, visions, descriptions of archetypes are simply articulations of global generalizations/idealizations and these articulations have to be made particular in each specific, contingent situation which leads to conflict that must be negotiated. The articulation of the global generalization is an abstraction from experience and can only be found in the experience of particularizing the generalization and functionalizing the idealization. So even with regard to the short term and rather repetitive events, planning activities will be problematic, although we would say in such restricted situations they remain useful, budgeting being an example.

Central to the complex responsive process perspective is the notion of emergence according to which global patterns continually emerge in local interaction and this means that they come about in the absence of global plans or designs, or if there are such global plans and designs they will not be operating as the cause of the global pattern that appears because that global pattern is emergent. So in these circumstances, any strategic planning, organizational leverage activities are largely fantasies whose function might largely be to form social defenses against anxiety. The problem with them as a defense is that they blinker people and if taken seriously can easily get in the way of more improvisational, spontaneous behavior. So it is our view that such activities are, in many ways, a distracting waste of time and could be discontinued with the benefits far outweighing any drawbacks. Instead of being planned, global patterns emerge in myriad local interactions and this is especially true for global patterns displaying any form of novelty. It becomes extremely important, then, to understand the largely improvisational nature of such ordinary local interaction. This does not mean that people are acting without intention or expectation. Those engaged in local interactions do have intentions, perhaps even plans, for their own local interaction, but the global patterns emerge in the interplay between all of their intentions/plans, and the interplay cannot be said to be planned so neither can the global pattern. Instead local interaction takes on the form of improvisational acting with a high degree of spontaneity. Such improvisation/spontaneous acting cannot be said to be planning although it does not mean that there is no intention on the part of those engaging in the improvisational local interaction. The relationship between the local and the global is explored in some detail in Stacey, 2005.

Outline of the book

The author of Chapter 2, Chris Mowles, is an independent consultant to organizations working in the area of aid to developing countries. The great majority of those working in various roles in the many government and non government organizations concerned with such development work clearly display a very obvious concern with values to do with alleviating poverty, emancipation and democracy – we can perhaps describe this ideology by the phrase "make poverty history". If there is any endeavor in which people can claim to be sharing the same values, one would have thought that this would be it. This makes Mowles' choice of aid agencies a particularly appropriate area to explore just how value motivation is expressed in ordinary work life. He takes a specific meeting with an official, in a specific government aid donor agency, in a specific country, relating to a project to do with improving drinking water supplies and sanitation. He then uses his narrative to explore just how value orientation is expressed in this local interaction. This may be a specific episode in a specific organization but it has general implications for organizations of all kinds in many situations. The chapter is concerned with how people find they must negotiate the *conflict* generated by jarring ideologies such as "making poverty history", on the one hand, and "managerialism" as the required form of governance, on the other hand. Such conflict inevitably means that people have to *compromise* one value or another. Although arising in a specific situation, in a specific place and time, this point has general significance for all organizations.

At the time of writing Chapter 3, Arnie Grant was the managing director of a division of a large services company. He was appointed to lead the negotiation of a major new labor contract with the Unions. The story of these negotiations provides an opportunity to reflect upon the nature of *conflict*, not just in labor contract negotiations, but in organizational life in general. Grant explores the literature on conflict in both sociology and organizational theory, describing how much of that literature understands conflict as a characteristic of antagonistic relationships between people. Prescriptions are then provided for dealing with different types of conflict to produce consensus and solve problems. Grant contrasts this way of thinking about conflict with that to be found in the theory of complex responsive processes of relating which draws on the views of Elias and Mead. Here, conflict is not understood simply in antagonist terms but is regarded as an inevitable aspect of all human relationships arising from the need to interpret generalized norms and idealized values in particular contingent situations and from the fact that human interdependence means that all human relationships are power relationships. This leads Grant to draw a distinction between what he calls polarized conflict, in which people take up fixed win–lose positions, and explorative conflict, in which they carry on talking about their differences and negotiating a way of going on together. He does not, however, see these as distinct types of human conflict, but as aspects of human relating that are never far from each other. So while, in Chapter 2, Mowles draws our attention to the nature of values and ideology as the basis for conflict, this chapter focuses our attention on the nature of conflict in the ordinary everyday lives of people in organizations.

In Chapter 4, Iver Drabæk, an independent consultant, describes the ethical issue arising in relation to an invitation to work as an auditor required to verify information provided by companies for a database of ethical companies. Drabæk draws attention to the potential conflict between his need to earn an income, on the one hand, and his misgivings about the principle of the audit itself and the adequacy of the budget made available to pay for the verification. His misgivings arise from his view that too many compromises had been made in the interest of making registration on the database attractive to companies. In his view, these compromises greatly diminished the usefulness of the audit in guiding the decisions of customers. However, he did approve of the idea in principle and he did need the income from the project. He too, therefore, was faced with compromises and decided to carry out the work. Drabæk takes the situation he faced and the struggle he had to make an ethical decision as a reflection of much wider patterns in the auditing and accountancy professions. He draws attention to the cult values of these professions which center on independence and objectivity. The values of independence/objectivity therefore come into conflict with the need to generate income, so creating situations in which some form of compromise becomes a practical necessity. Drabæk's main concern in this chapter is that of how we are to think about the matter of compromise in professional and organizational life.

For some time now, those engaging in the activity of leading in changing, learning organizations, as well as those writing about such activities, have made strong links between effective leadership and a leader's capacity for self-mastery, based on values. Such self-mastery is sometimes described as "ruthless compassion". However, notions of self-mastery and ruthless compassion are generally described in rather harmonious, even mystical terms. It is rare to find explorations of just what it actually means to master oneself and the pain that this might involve. It is even rarer to find explorations of just what it actually means to be ruthless as in ruthless compassion. The author of Chapter 5, Martin Daly, is a priest and the principal of a Catholic school in Ireland. The story he tells in this chapter is about the ruthless action he felt compelled to take to remove a non-performing teacher from his school. He writes about the intentional, value-driven refusal to compromise. Previous chapters in this volume have focused attention on values, the inevitable conflict that arises when the idealizations of value are made functional in contingent situations and the compromises this so often entails. This chapter focuses our attention on how and why the commitment to value may actually call for a "no compromise" response. However, Daly argues that the ethical "no compromise" response requires attitudes as rigorously reflexive as the kind of ethical compromise Drabæk wrote about in Chapter 4.

In Chapter 6, Stephen Billing, an independent consultant, describes his involvement in a change management project in a high technology company. The central issue, then, has to do with conflicting views about how an effective change management project is to be conducted. Billing deals with the conflict by apparently agreeing to what the client wants but keeps open the option of influencing the project in another direction once it commences. As in previous chapters, conflict immediately gives rise to the various possibilities for compromise and, as before, this immediately raises issues of values and of ethics. Is it ethical to continue working on a project one fundamentally disagrees with? Is it ethical to assuage one's unease about doing so by retaining an undisclosed intention to change the way of working as the project develops? These are the questions Billing deals with in this chapter. In the course of dealing with these questions he explores the relationship between the techniques of organizational development and propaganda.

References

Allen, P. M. (1998a) "Evolving complexity in social science", in Altman, G. and Koch, W. A. (eds.) *Systems: New Paradigms for the Human Sciences*, New York: Walter de Gruyter.

Allen, P. M. (1998b) "Modeling complex economic evolution", in Schweitzer, F. and Silverberg, G. (eds.) *Selbstorganization*, Berlin: Dunker and Humbolt.

Dalal, F. (1998) *Taking the Group Seriously*, London: Jessica Kingsley.

Damasio, A. R. (1994) *Descartes' Error: Emotion, Reason and the Human Brain*, London: Picador.

Damasio, A. R. (1999) *The Feeling of What Happens: Body and Emotion in the Making of Consciousness*, London: Heinemann.

Dewey, J. (1934) *A Common Faith*, New Haven, CT: Yale University Press.

Elias, N. ([1939], 2000) *The Civilizing Process*, Oxford: Blackwell.

Fonseca, J. (2001) *Complexity and Innovation in Organizations*, London: Routledge.

Griffin, D. (2002) *The Emergence of Leadership: Linking Self-organization and Ethics*, London: Routledge.

Griffin, D. and Stacey, R. (eds.) (2005) *Complexity and the Experience of Leading Organizations*, London: Routledge.

Jackson, M. C. (2000) *Systems Approaches to Management*, New York: Kluwer.

Joas, H. (2000) *The Genesis of Values*, Cambridge: Polity Press.

Kauffman, S. A. (1995) *At Home in the Universe*, New York: Oxford University Press.

Mead, G. H. (1934), *Mind Self and Society*, Chicago: Chicago University Press.

Mead, G. H. (1932) "Scientific method and the moral sciences", *International Journal of Ethics*, 33: pp. 229–47.

Midgley, G. (2000) *Systemic Intervention: Philosophy, Methodology, and Practice*, New York: Kluwer.

Mintzberg, H., Ahlstrand, B. and Lampel, J. (1998) *Strategy Safari: A guided tour through the wilds of strategic management*, New York: Free Press.

Ray, T. S. (1992) "An approach to the synthesis of life", in Langton, G. C., Taylor, C., Doyne-Farmer, J. and Rasmussen, S. (eds.) *Artificial Life II, Santa Fe Institute, Studies in the Sciences of Complexity, Volume 10*, Reading MA: Addison-Wesley.

Senge, P. M. (1990) *The Fifth Discipline: The Art of Practice of the Learning Organization*, New York: Doubleday.

Shaw, P. (2002) *Changing Conversation in Organizations*, London: Routledge.

Shaw, P. and Stacey, R. (eds.) (2006) *Experiencing Risk, Spontaneity and Improvisation in Organizational Change: Working Live*, London: Routledge.

Stacey, R. (2001) *Complex Responsive Processes in Organizations: Learning and Knowledge Creation*, London: Routledge.

Stacey, R. (ed.) (2005) *Experiencing Emergence in Organizations: Local Interaction and the Emergence of Global Pattern*, London: Routledge.

Stacey, R. (2007) *Strategic Management and Organizational Dynamics: The Challenge of Complexity*, London: Pearson Education (5th Edition).

Stacey, R. and Griffin, D. (eds.) (2005) *A Complexity Perspective on Researching Organizations: Taking Experience Seriously*, London: Routledge.

Stacey, R. and Griffin, D. (eds.) (2006) *Complexity and the Experience of Managing in Public Sector Organizations*, London: Routledge.

Stacey, R., Griffin, D. and Shaw, P. (2000) *Complexity and Management: Fad or Radical Challenge to Systems Thinking?* London: Routledge.

Streatfield, P. (2001) *The Paradox of Control in Organizations*, London: Routledge.

Editors' introduction to Chapter 2

The author of this chapter, Chris Mowles, is an independent consultant to organizations working in the area of aid to developing countries. He focuses attention on an issue which, for some years now, has attracted the attention of a great many leaders and managers in organizations of all kinds, ranging from major international banks, oil companies and public sector services to small local charities. That issue has to do with the role that values play in organizational life generally and in the quality, efficiency and effectiveness of organizational change and improvement. There has been a growing awareness of the powerful motivating effects of the values people are inspired by and the importance of the self control which belief in values instills. This interest has been most visibly expressed in various prescriptions for designing values, usually seen as the role of leaders, and converting organizational members to believe in, and act upon, the shared values expressed in value statements, missions and visions. The result of this effort has been highly generalized and idealized propositional statements, often provoking cynicism on the part of organizational members, with little evidence that it achieves much. What is lacking is the exploration of what we actually mean by human values and what it means to act according to values in ordinary, everyday life in organizations. This is what Mowles seeks to address in this chapter through reflecting on his work in organizations concerned with aiding development in the less developed countries of the world.

The great majority of those working in various roles in the many government and non government organizations concerned with such development work clearly display a very obvious concern with values to do with emancipation, democracy and alleviating poverty – we can perhaps describe this ideology by the phrase "make poverty history". If there is any endeavor in which people can claim to be sharing the same values, one would have thought that this would be it. This makes Mowles' choice of aid agencies a particularly appropriate area to explore just how value motivation is expressed in ordinary work life. He takes a specific meeting with a specific official, in a specific government aid donor agency, relating to a project to do with improving drinking water supplies and sanitation. He then uses his narrative to explore just how value orientation is expressed in this local interaction. This may be a specific episode in a specific organization but it has general implications for organizations of all kinds.

The official that Mowles meets is charged with monitoring the performance of the organizations that her own government donor organization is funding so that her organization can account, ultimately to the tax payer, for the proper, effective use of public funds. Performance is to be accounted for in terms of "outcomes" and "deliverables" to do with improving the lot of those for whom the money is being donated. This perfectly reasonable, simple sounding requirement turns out to be anything but simple. It amounts, in effect, to an ideology consisting of values to do with honesty, transparency and efficiency combined with norms to do with preparing generalized plans, measuring outcomes, and keeping to budget limits and time frames. This ideology can be described as "managerialism", the belief that rational techniques of management will produce better outcomes. Mowles' narrative immediately makes it clear that in ordinary, everyday life people in aid agencies find that they have no choice but to somehow negotiate the *conflict* generated by what turns out in many ways to be jarring ideologies of "making poverty history" and "managerialism". Such conflict inevitably means that people have to *compromise* one value or another. Although arising in a specific situation, this point has general significance for all organizations. The view, now so taken for granted, that organizations will be more effective if appropriate organizational values are designed and shared, comes to look quite naive as soon as one recognizes the inevitable conflicts and compromises which will be generated when people interact on the basis of their actual values. One perfectly valid ideology, such as "managerialism", will inevitably come into conflict with other perfectly valid ideologies, such as "make poverty history". And the only way to carry on together, as opposed to breaking apart into factions, will be to negotiate ongoing compromises which inevitably reflect the power relations between the various groupings of people involved.

In reflecting on his meeting with the Donor agency official, Mowles is struck by how the managerialist way in which both of them are required to work, if the funds for the aid project are to be made available, requires them and others involved to detach themselves, in important ways, from the very values of poverty alleviation that draw them to the work in the first place. The managerialist accounting for "deliverables" in a highly generalized way takes no account of the messy contingencies of actually doing the work. The result is accusation and counteraccusation leading to conflicts which actually delay and inhibit the work of the project. The required compromises, if anything at all is to be done on the project, take the form of subtly subverting the managerialist agenda while paying lip service to it. Mowles points to how this power struggle with conflicting values, expressed in the creation, translation and destabilization of interpretations and narratives, is actually reflected in the processes of self formation of all involved. Far from values being abstract propositions which can be designed by some and shared by others, we can see how the narrative experience of power relations as value and value conflict is at the heart of what it means for each of us to be a person.

This brings Mowles to the matter of mutual recognition. Recognition can be based on "rights", such as contractual arrangements, which generate personal self respect, and/or on solidarity, which arises in belonging to a community oriented to shared conceptions of goals which nevertheless recognize differences, all yielding personal self esteem. The result is an irresolvable paradox:

> In the relationship between Donor A and NGO B, defined as a legal contract, there is an assumption that there is an agreement between parties on rationally agreed norms; the contingent exceptions of context, i.e. culture and ways of working, are currently not being viewed as admissible reasons for failure to adhere to the contract as specified. In signing this contract NGO B has aspired to be a fully recognized citizen with all the respect that will accompany this recognition within the community of development agencies and donors, but it is a community with a particular set of values and assumptions about the way that development can work. The paradox for NGO B is that the relationships of solidarity they have built up with their partners are negated by the very contract that they have signed, which recognizes only standardized development outputs, or "deliverables".

2 Finding room for values in required ways of working

Values, power, conflict and compromise in aid agencies

Chris Mowles

In this chapter, I am concerned with the themes of power and values in the context of working with international Non Government Organizations (NGOs) and aid donors. In describing my experience I have bumped up against a series of paradoxes in the work that I have undertaken with others and this too has become a theme that I want to explore further. So I will attempt a critique of the development literature and then go on to explore the similarities and differences between the ideas expressed in more mainstream development thinking and an approach that the theory of complex responsive processes of relating might take toward the same issues.

The formalities and informalities of project management

I have worked with a British NGO in Asia, which I will call NGO B, for the last two and half years, helping to prepare for taking on a contract with a large donor agency, which I will call Donor A, and have worked with NGO B subsequently as an intermittent support whilst they implement it. The contract is to last for five years and constitutes an attempt to scale up by a factor of five work that had been successfully undertaken up to that point between NGO B and local NGOs it calls "partners". Instead of spending £500,000 a year they aimed to spend £2.5 million a year connecting poor communities to clean water supplies and helping them build latrines. International NGOs (INGOs) very often do not work operationally in the countries where they are located but fund local organizations to do so. Their role, then, is as critical friend, support, trainer, and coach. They undertake what they term "capacity building" with partners, by which they mean enhancing their skills and capacities to undertake the work that they mutually agree upon. In this instance, NGO B have taken on a contract with Donor A to scale up their work delivered through partners in urban and rural areas with the aim of reaching three million beneficiaries.

I had been asked by the Asia Regional Manager of NGO B, who was located in the UK, to visit country B and support the NGO B team there because of mounting pressures within that office and between the NGO B team and local partners, as well as between Donor A and NGO B, all perceived to be the result of the new contract with Donor A. At the time of my visit, the staff of NGO B were a year into their contract and had passed through the initial phase of the project called the "inception phase", where they are supposed to have done all the necessary hiring of new staff, training of partners, and planning and the writing of policy papers. Staff within Donor A and local partners were concerned about delays in progress, and some employees within NGO B were protesting about the perceived difference in management style that undertaking the new project had brought about. For some progress was too slow, for others it was too fast and was failing to take enough staff members along with the changes. At the same time, there was a new indigenous Country Representative in NGO B, who had been promoted from within; he had been party to the setting up of the new project but had not been in charge of it. Equally, all the staff within Donor A who had helped shape the initial project had moved on to other countries and the project was now being managed by newcomers who had not known the project from the beginning.

In my meetings in London and in country B, I became aware of an increasing level of what might best be described as panic amongst senior managers about NGO B's perceived failure to produce what were termed "deliverables". From the Regional Manager's perspective, based in London, everything seemed to be taking an inordinate amount of time and he himself had been involved in meetings with Donor A in London to explain away the delays. The partners were chafing in two different ways; they wanted to be allowed to get on with the work, but felt that NGO B was being too perfectionist about what had to be in place before the work started, and they also experienced managers in NGO B as being mired in organizational changes brought on by attempts to adapt to what they thought Donor A required of them. Partners were not always sure in what voice employees in NGO B were talking to them; as NGO B or as representatives of the Donor A. We had a number of conversations about contracts and contract compliance, the meaning of partnership and the stresses and strains that this new set of expectations was creating.

The background

Donor A is a medium-sized civil service bureaucracy which privileges paperwork and policy as a way of working. At the center of Donor A's project development methodology is a logical framework approach or log frame, which is in essence a cybernetic system, describing milestones and outputs for the whole five-year project. Progress is tracked on a continuous basis against these milestones, and it was this tracking process which had caused alarm in Donor A, in both its UK and Country B offices, because the project was falling behind schedule. Moreover, Donor A sets broad social objectives for its projects which have to be supported by comprehensive documentation. So NGO B was obliged to produce papers on how the project would also support gender relations, equity, the eradication of poverty, as well as promoting good governance. There were a number of ironies around this way of working. First, staff from Donor A had themselves contributed to the delay in the project by refusing to sign off on some of the paperwork which they considered to be of insufficient quality. This had resulted in a three-month delay the previous autumn. Second, in insisting that NGO B was light on expertise, staff from Donor A had persuaded NGO B to appoint two senior advisers, one on poverty, equity and gender, and the other on governance. Adviser posts are very much a civil service creation. They have no line management responsibility as such but are deemed to be senior posts, their purpose being to produce policy from which good development practice is supposed to flow. Not only did the two new senior posts create conflict within NGO B about what their purpose was and how they fitted into the hierarchy, but they also contributed to overheads, about which Donor A was now beginning to complain.

In response to the panic amongst senior managers about the perceived lack of progress, the person responsible for NGO B within Donor A in country B had begun trying to exert more and more pressure. This pressure manifested itself in her asking questions about how much time various members of NGO B staff were spending on Donor A-funded work to the extent of calling into question their leaving the country on NGO B business, and demanding that NGO B demonstrate productivity improvements. This form of coercion was creating resentment within the senior management team of NGO B, who nonetheless began pressuring their own partners to work faster; the partners themselves were mildly affronted, feeling that they had been ready to work faster all along.

Meeting the Country B representative

I eventually got to meet the Donor A representative toward the end of my visit to Country B and discovered her to be a young British woman originating from that country, far removed from my experience of the white, middle-aged men who were responsible for initiating the project. She was bright and personable and showed herself to have a keen interest in the success of the project. After the initial preliminaries and explanations of what I was there to do, I began to test out with her how possible it was to explore some of the contradictions that I had experienced so far: NGO B was being held responsible for the performance of its partners over which it had minimum control; Donor A was partly responsible for the delay that it was criticizing; the log frame is a planning tool and a best guess at what scaling up to that degree might mean, yet she was applying pressure as though these projections were entirely reasonable.

Although she accepted many of these points, and moved visibly from her starting position, admitting that she had been "demanding" and agreeing to meet the partners face to face rather than working just through NGO B, she nonetheless responded fairly defensively. On the one hand, she said she could only expect what was "reasonable", and on the other hand, she argued in a way that I experience many middle managers arguing in large bureaucracies, that NGO B should demonstrate how it is "adding value" to the enterprise and could demonstrate effectiveness and value for money. There would be an opportunity to "finalize" the log frame and NGO B had, after all, signed a contract. She said that since she had not been involved with the project from the start, she felt she could be more detached. This was something she expected NGO B to be able to do too, to stand back from its partners and be more objective. She also mentioned that water and sanitation was just one of her areas of responsibility, since she was responsible for energy and transportation too. She simply did not have time to follow the detail of the project and that is one of the reasons why Donor A had contracted NGO B to do this.

I could see toward the end of an hour that she was getting restless and that she was beginning to make gestures and signs that she was not going to sit there comfortably for much longer. I took the lead from her cue and told her that I would not take up much more of her time. Just before I rose to leave, she commented on my business card, which we had exchanged in formal fashion at the beginning of the meeting. "I notice from your business card that you live just down the road from me. I was born and brought up in Oxford, and my parents still live there." It was like a dam bursting. In a very short timescale we exchanged where she had gone to school, where my own children go to school, and what had happened during the last election to the local MP. On the one hand she was clearly conscious of the fact that the "neutral" civil servant façade had slipped, yet on the other she clearly could not stop herself. She told me about how she had trained as an engineer, how she had practiced engineering herself in the developing world and how she had a passionate interest in reaching the largest number of people with this current NGO B project.

By the time we had completed our walk to the front door the formalities were more or less resumed, yet I was conscious that something significant had happened. Through the interstices of her role and the way that she had been trained to think and talk about development projects, her real passion for the detail of the work shone through. And not just about the work, but about life in Oxford and politics in general and I began to recognize her as a person in her own right. We had both experienced her being indiscreet. And yet she had been sitting on this enthusiasm for the duration of the meeting. I wonder whether there would have been circumstances where she would have not shown it at all, and how different the meeting would have been if she had made the connection at the beginning of the meeting. It was clearly more than just a job to her; she was doing it because it aligned with her values and the difference that she wanted to make through her work.

The nature of values

Joas (2000), following Dewey (1934), says that the experience of value is the paradox of voluntary compulsion, providing an uplifting meaning to life. Values are, at the same time freely chosen and felt not to be of our own positing. Values contrast with norms which are obligatory and constraining, providing moral criteria for assessing what ought to be done. Joas compares and contrasts these by describing them as the difference between the good (what I/we consider to be good, driven by my/our values) and the right, which is what the majority of reasonable people would consider to be the right. This idea of paradox at the heart of values will become central to my argument and I will be looking to see what other authors make of the same concept.

What I experienced in my encounter with this Donor A employee was very different from what I had expected from other people's descriptions of the way that she had been working, although I had experienced that side too. I have begun to wonder how such a person, who has obviously struggled herself to do well, who has experienced water and sanitation work directly in developing countries and who cares about what she was doing could come to work in a way that people experienced as bewildering and oppressive. I wonder how much of herself she had to hold in whilst doing her job and where she would go for an outlet for her enthusiasms and her value judgments about the work that she was doing. I wonder also how constrained she felt by Donor A's norms and how much freedom she could find for the expression of her values in her work. I wonder how she dealt with these conflicts and the compromises they demanded of her.

It strikes me that it was partly the way that she was required to do her job that kept her so detached from the emotional charge and engagement that I experienced at the end of our meeting. Because she is so busy with three big thematic briefs and because, partly in recognition of this, Donor A contracts out the day to day management of projects to third parties, such as NGO B, or even to myself as a consultant, she is removed from direct contact with the contingent nature of messy development work in context. For nearly nine months she had not visited the field, had not had seen with her own eyes, heard with her own ears, the difficulties of what was being attempted. In the absence of direct experience, all that she had to fall back on were the log frame and the policy documents. I noticed how narrow the discussion becomes when it turns into a question and answer session about why the "deliverables" have not been produced to time, and how I myself have allowed contractors such as Donor A to escape the difficulties of undertaking development by absorbing them myself, and as an intermediary, simply passing on a polished product.

I can see that we are both, Donor A employee and I, trapped in the dynamic that we contribute to and are formed by. However, in the past I have had a much clearer defeatist sense of victimhood about my situation as a consultant; it was easy to portray my practice as being me against the big donors and their ways of working. My choices were either to accept a contract and undertake the work as I thought the contractor wanted me to do it, in a way that I often found incredibly constraining, or not accept the contract at all. On reflection and from experience, however, I can see that there are far more options than that. From the above narrative and other experiences, I have realized that, although we come at this from different places, employees from Donor A and I are in many ways in the same situation, struggling, to a greater or lesser extent, to find room for our values in the way that we are required to work. There can be as much that unites as divides us. We all have to make compromises.

What becomes intriguing, then, is what it is about the way that international development is undertaken, the narratives and expectations about what constitutes professional practice that so shapes the ways of working as to limit and constrain what we talk about and the way we talk about it. It is this that I will start to investigate first and try to locate myself and my own practice within it.

Development discourses

There is a growing voice in development literature that is beginning to draw attention to the disjuncture between the specifying of what needs to be done and the doing of it, between policy and practice. For example David Mosse, an anthropologist and development practitioner, has recently (2005) written what he describes as an ethnographic study of ten years' involvement with a development project in India in which he draws attention to the growing gap between donors' infatuation with policy work and its complete removal from the realities on the ground:

> The policy-oriented staff of donor agencies [like Donor A] are themselves increasingly removed from the contingencies of development. But at the same time ... aid policy has become more managerial. Its ends – the quantified reduction of poverty or ill health – have narrowed, but its means have diversified to the management of more and more; financial and political systems and civil society. A unipolar global political order renews confidence in rational design and social engineering ... The paradox is that "high managerialism" actually controls less and less. It privileges policy over practice ... More than ever, international development is about generating consensus on approaches and framing models that link investment to outcomes, rather than implementation modalities. Questions of implementation are somebody else's problem.
>
> (Mosse, 2005: 237)

Mosse argues that projects can be successful despite, rather than because of, the policy context that frames them, and illustrates how policy workers in donor agencies, consultants such as myself, and even some project workers, are often remote from the network of relationships and the social, economic and historical context in which they are working. In this reference he also starts to explore what he refers to as paradox, noting the contradictory movements of donor bureaucracies wanting to control more and more and yet becoming further and further removed from the everyday experience of managing. I suggest that, rather than drawing attention to paradox, which I explore later, Mosse is merely pointing out a contradiction, an irony that on the one hand managerialism wants to control more, whereas the reality is that managers can control less and less.

He discusses how conversations within donor agencies are about stabilizing the favored representations of how things are said to be working and about garnering the necessary political support for those representations:

> If one problem with the assertion of policy over practice is the subjugation of certain positive outcomes; a second is the perpetuation of false models, simplifications and development illusions. In the competitive market for success it is difficult for dependent agencies *not* to portray their actions as achievements in terms of currently favored models. The cost of breaking ranks is high and public disputes over meaning and interpretation are rare.
>
> (Mosse, 2005: 235)

In drawing attention to the power dynamic and the difficulty of opposing the growing convergence of thinking about how best to do development, Mosse helps re-problematize relationships that can sometimes become occluded in technical vocabulary and legal representations. For example, staff in both NGO B and NGO B UK felt uncomfortable that they had signed a contract with Donor A and obliged their organizations to deliver the outcomes as specified. My experience of them was that they felt powerless to argue their case, to set out some of the legitimate reasons for delays and to admit some of the less legitimate ones. My argument is that some of their feelings of powerlessness relate to their inability to find legitimate expression for their values in dialogue with Donor A because the latter *demands the same detachment from values* from those whom they contract as they do from their own employees. This is an area I particularly want to explore as this chapter unfolds because I have found myself caught up in the same dynamic as a consultant practitioner, and have felt myself silenced in situations where the obvious things for me to draw attention to became covered over with an instrumental discussion about targets or outcomes. It is important to be able to talk about *both*, the modalities of what we need to talk about in order to deliver the project *and* what that means to us as interlocutors. My experience as a contractor is that the former often drives out the latter.

Another important development of Mosse's approach, which is also to be found in other writers such as Eyben (2003), and Cleaver (2002), in contradistinction to the Donor A member of staff's call for NGO B to be detached from its partners, is to rehabilitate the subjective, and to include the actions and perspectives of the author as an object of study in what is being described. Not only does this new cohort of development commentators take themselves seriously as actors in the narrative that they are writing about but they are interested in the day to day, local actions of ordinary project staff and beneficiaries to show how:

> Subordinate actors in development, tribal villagers, fieldworkers, office staff, even project managers and their bosses in relation to donors, create everyday spheres of action autonomous from the organizing policy models, but at the same time work actively to sustain those same models – the dominant interpretations – because it is in their interest to do so ... It will

become clear how, paradoxically, the practices of project workers erode the models that they also work to reinstate as representations.

(Mosse, 2005: 10)

Mosse is drawing attention to a simultaneous, paradoxical dynamic that occurs in projects where actors both sustain and undermine the narratives that describe the work being undertaken and in doing so he is keen to pursue not whether, but *how*, development projects work. By describing the work in this way he tries to distinguish himself from two other schools of commentary on approaches to development. He argues that there are three schools writing about international development and the organizations that undertake it; the instrumental school; the critical school, which takes instrumentalism and mainstream development to task; and Mosse's own school, which is a progressive ethnographic approach that I will call the social anthropological school, which criticizes both. In a later section, I will start to explore what the theory of complex responsive processes of relating might add to the mix.

Though they are more focused on development as a theory than the organizational and management consequences that underpin it, the instrumentalist writers (Fowler, 1997, 2000; Edwards and Hulme, 1992, 1995), although thoughtful and critical, nevertheless promote the idea of INGO performance through management and planning techniques. It is important to bear in mind that any categorization is going to cover over important nuances and differences; I would not want to imply that the instrumental school is in any way blind to some of the broader issues to do with power and values that I have outlined above. For example, in a recent essay on NGOs and social change, Edwards and Sen criticize INGOs for having forgotten their values:

The claim that development NGOs are explicitly "values-based" organizations is an article of faith these days. However, there is less evidence that NGOs put these values into practice in their organizational structures and behavior, or even that they are clear what their core values are.

(Edwards and Sen, 2002: 47)

And I will return later to what their prescriptions would be for bringing issues of power and values back to the fore. However, writers in the instrumental school spend time exploring how the dominant managerialism can be applied in the international development context.

In the critical school we would find commentators, broadly speaking from a Marxist and/or particularly French Post-modernist tradition, promoting a contrary view that development has become a form of imperialism (Escobar, 1995; Esteva and Prakash, 1998; Cowen and Shenton, 1996), or that management methodologies in use in donor agencies are a necessary accompaniment to economic liberalism (Cooke and Kothari, 2001). In addition it would also be important to mention the humanist critics of the instrumental school, principal among them being Robert Chambers (1997, 2002), because of their substantial contribution to thinking about participation and participatory methodologies which aim to challenge the orthodox power balances. In the third category, the anthropological school, I will place Mosse, Eyben and Cleaver.

I want to stay with these three broad ways of thinking about the management of development to see how useful they are for understanding my experience in country B. In particular I want to explore how they represent the nexus of power and values.

Instrumentalism

In returning to my experience in country B, I would want to argue that the person I was dealing with in Donor A was constrained to an extent within the instrumental position taken up by her agency, but it was one that she herself momentarily tried to subvert. This might be an example of what Mosse alluded to in the quotation above where workers in the project both subvert and uphold the narrative about the project at the same time in their daily dealings. If we consider this situation in context with an over-stretched member of staff in Donor A from a minority background, and a woman trying to make an impact in her own institution, there can be little wonder that, in the formal context of an interview about NGO B's performance, there was no room for challenging the orthodoxies of the managerialist approach. The vocabulary of what has become known as managerialism, with its emphasis on compliance and "best practice", does not often invite investigation and can operate according to an occluded organizational logic. Although nominally about learning, the project is also about Donor A being able to make credible representations to the relevant Minister in the home government that money has been well spent and that a specified number of beneficiaries have been lifted out of poverty. Instrumentalism finds it difficult to entertain other discourses. Yet it is difficult to know whether it was through the interaction with me, perhaps the invitation to reflect on the role that she was playing as project manager, perhaps by my expressing points of view that had not been expressed to date by NGO B staff through their lack of assertiveness, that she could recognize herself in what she was saying. In an instant of doubt and self-reflection the power balance had shifted slightly.

The instrumental approach is not blind to power issues; adherents are capable of mounting a critical review of gender relations, or the structural causes of poverty, for example. But it is rare to experience an analysis that starts from the level of personal interaction with others; discourses on power in the instrumental context tend to be at the meta level. A cursory review of Fowler's books, for example, reveals little analysis of power in inter-relational terms. Quarles Van Ufford *et al.* (2003) accuse instrumentalists of unbounded, a-historical and artificial optimism; the authors point to the fact that development management makes completely unrealistic claims that through the proliferation of managerial instruments societies can be re-engineered top to bottom for the good.

The confidence in rational design and social engineering has never been greater, and the policy concepts applied reflect a growing sophistication of management, which is able to absorb and deflect challenges. Bottom-up, and "participatory" development approaches, which spread within mainstream development agencies in tandem with "results-oriented management", often serve the instrumental needs of program delivery rather than reviving a critical politics of development (Quarles Van Ufford *et al.*, 2003: 6–7).

My guess would be that issues of power within Donor A as an agency would be just as difficult to draw attention to as would be power relations between Donor A and NGO B, and Donor A employee and myself. Organizations idealize their values to such an extent that to stray from them would be to invite exclusion or censure.

The critical school

Next, I want to turn to the critical school and two thinkers who are central to them to see how much of a contribution to my understanding of power and values they might make. The theme that I will look at in particular is the one set out by Mosse that working in development projects is a struggle over the creation, translation and destabilization of interpretations and narratives about what is happening.

The influence of French post-modernists, particularly Foucault and Derrida, are pervasive in the critical development literature, especially the idea that power arises in the struggle for dominance of one narrative over another, or that the process of exclusion and inclusion is an act of violence. This is what Parfitt (2002) argues in a book about postmodernism and development where he attempts to rescue Derrida from what he considers to be the twin poles of foundationalism and relativism. By foundationalism, he means an essentialism that frames things in terms of absolutes. He is here making the argument that the critical school has over-egged their case in attacking instrumentalism, and uses post-modernist writers to make a more nuanced but still critical case against development:

> Our analysis of deconstruction (*Derrida and Levinas*) has shown that, contrary to the prejudices of many observers, it is not a relativistic discourse at all. In fact, of the various theoretical structures we have examined, it is probably the most successful in dealing with the dilemma of foundationalism versus relativism. In formulating our theories and analytical positions we have to institute closure, this being the only access to truth that we have. However, it must always be remembered that in making a closure, we inevitably commit the violence of making exclusions, and our exclusions return to haunt us. It follows from this that the course of least violence is to try and remain open to alterity, to welcome the other.
>
> (Parfitt, 2002: 115)

The term "radical alterity" is one that Derrida used to describe the interdependence of concepts that are linked in a binary fashion, say speech and writing, where, although one is usually privileged over the other, their radical interdependence will mean that the less privileged concept will return to destabilize the privileged. In bringing about "closure" then, recognizing this rather than that, choosing this rather than that, we are doing violence to otherness. What is useful in Parfitt's interpretation of the structuralist position is the encouragement to be open to otherness that the staff member in Donor A, for good reasons and bad, appeared to find difficult, and equally what I might have witnessed in Derrida's terms is an example of alterity where the worker from Donor A temporarily destabilized her own instrumental position because of the exclusions she had made to adopt it. However, where Derrida's position seems to stretch too far, when viewed from my experience in country B, is in the implication that the privileging of one concept over another amounts to violence, and that the destabilization process happens inevitably, curiously without human agency. It is true that staff from NGO B had experienced the Donor A's intervention in the project to be hugely discomfiting; they had not yet located their voice to engage with the premises of what was being argued against them; they themselves had not been able to argue a position of "alterity". However, to describe the relationship of power that exists between donor and recipient and equating it with violence draws the picture far more starkly than I experienced it in country B, where a degree of gentle probing did bring about some movement, a minimal recognition that there were other ways of perceiving things and other ways of behaving.

Foucault, another favorite of the critical school of development, can be equally monolithic, or in Derrida's terms "totalizing", in his analysis of power, as this example from the essay entitled *Truth and Power* (1984) shows:

> "Truth" is to be understood as a system of ordered procedures for the production, regulation, distribution, circulation, and operation of statements. "Truth" is linked in a circular relation with systems of power which produce and sustain it, and to effects of power and truth which it induces and which extends it. A "regime" of truth.... It's not a matter of emancipating truth from every system of power ... but of detaching the power of truth from the forms of hegemony, social, economic, and cultural within which it operates at the current time.
>
> (Foucault, 1984: 75)

From my experience of working as a consultant with donor and development agencies I would not want to underestimate the difficulty of arguing against the orthodox discourse concerning the way that development should take place. As Mosse pointed out above, "the cost of breaking ranks is high". However, to describe the relationship between donors and the organizations they fund as a kind of hegemony does not seem to me to do justice to the daily, hourly acts of subversion carried out by individuals both within and outside the "regime", and by the interaction between individuals that destabilize the dominant discourse. Moreover, for Foucault, the concept of power seems to be a thing, an *it*, which is lodged in social, economic and cultural systems that needs to be wrested from them. For me, Foucault's concept of power, as with Derrida's, is curiously reified, disembodied and static, removed from the day to day activities of human beings. And as Burkitt (1999) points out, Foucault's concept of power borrows heavily from Nietszche and relies on a Darwinian interpretation of human exist-ence as a recurring, violent struggle for domination. What this leaves out, as it does also for Derrida, is the possibility of creative human exchange, which, despite the obvious power imbalances, can create new possibilities other than one side triumphing over the other. In country B, I had no intention of meeting Donor A staff member and wresting power from her so that it passed to me, and yet, curiously, in our interaction a destabilization did take place.

The social anthropological school

The effect of the post-modernists is widespread, however, and Mosse too seems influenced by them in his portrayal of power and exclusion as an act of violence:

> The point is that modern development policy, which appears as rational abstraction separate from the social order it governs ... can be shown to be historically grounded in particular interests and events, contingencies, vio-lences and exclusions. The apparent logic, universality and coherence of these ideas, and the expertise and rational design they call forth, are not inherent but produced through the messiness of contingent practice which succeeds in concealing social practice by effecting the separation of ideas and their objects.
>
> (Mosse, 2005: 246)

Mosse's narrative is strong on the contingent and specific nature of development work and he reinstitutes the author/observer, as ethnographer, back into the picture. In doing so he reframes their status from objective, scientific observers who work in a value-free environment, and he centralizes the day to day practice of individuals working together. In this sense he separates himself from the instrumentalists, who still strive to impose a sense of order on a chaotic develop-ment world and work to stabilize narratives about what is happening on the ground, often without even being part of what is happening, by contracting out the task to others such as myself. They foster the concept of detachment and objectivity without being alive to the subjectivity of their own positions. Mosse also draws attention to the fact that both the instrumental school and the critical school fall into the same trap of essentializing or trivializing what they would intend to criticize. Cleaver (2002) makes a similar point about Chambers' humanism, accusing him of idealizing the knowledge of the poor:

> Positive views of culture tend towards a profound foundationalism about local communities and their inhabitants. For example, in the writings of Robert Chambers, a moral value is attributed to the knowledge, attitudes and practices of the poor, the task of development being to release their

potential to live these out.… Is there not a danger of swinging from one untenable position ("we know best") to an equally untenable and damaging one ("they know best")?

(Cleaver, 2002: 233)

Mosse puts forward the argument that although the position of the critical school can sometimes read like the obverse of the instrumental approach, they are simply two sides of the same coin. And he tries to make a separate space for a social anthropological and ethnographic approach. However, although he touches on power and the difficulty of undermining the dominant narratives, Mosse's argument is still essentially heavily influenced by a post-modern analysis of power as a struggle between competing discourses. In this sense his model is still abstracted from the day-to-day interaction of human beings. He also conflates, as does Foucault, the concepts of violence and power and writes about them as one and the same phenomenon. Understanding power does involve some judgment about the relationship of dominance, but this is not the same thing as assuming that violence is an integral part of the dynamic.

The struggle over value positions

The context of international development is a highly values-charged environment – actors within it are not only trying to do good, to make a difference, they are also trying to develop ways of working and ways of describing the doing of good in the alleviation of poverty and suffering. Conversations about development take place against this backdrop, what Charles Taylor (1991) calls "significant horizons", on a daily basis. What I mean here, drawing on Taylor, is that people who work in international development define what they do against a backdrop of moral concern about the injustice and the unacceptability of poverty and suffering in the developing world. Their work is judged by the community of practitioners to be of worth in the context of these horizons, the very same horizons which informed the genesis of development organizations in the first place and which are still a motivating factor for many of the people who work in them. Discussion about what kind of intervention makes the most difference becomes more charged because there seems to be so much at stake.

In the way that each of the schools of thought describe the interaction between human beings, between the developed world and the less developed world that we have come to understand as "development", there begins to emerge a way of presenting the nature of the ethical encounter, the struggle over value positions between the actors. The authors are themselves aware of the ethical problems that emerge and present a very different way of understanding them. Their way of seeing the world contains within it a prescription for changing it and turns in particular on the relations between the self and others.

For example, Edwards and Sen (2002), writing from within an instrumentalist position, are aware of the slippage between overtly value-driven organizations and their practice and see as a remedy a call for personal transformation:

It is fascinating to recognize that the core of religious teaching concerns our feelings towards each other – a deeply social statement as much as it is profoundly personal. But to love our neighbors as ourselves, we must come to understand our inner being, to recognize that in our deepest essence we are compassionate, capable of giving love and worthy of receiving it.

(Edwards and Sen, 2002: 43)

I put forward the argument above that the writers within the instrumentalist position generally have a weak grasp of the power relations between individuals and usually describe power at the meta level, as being about gender inequality or social exclusion. Edwards and Sen are less interested in issues of power relating, but in our mutual feelings for each other. There seems here to be an unacknowledged paradox at the heart of the reference that although both authors call for a greater recognition of interdependence and decry selfishness, their solution lies in the direction of personal transformation and discovering one's "inner essence". The authors never explore this potentially generative paradox of transforming the self with a view to transforming others. There seems to be no clear way of bridging the inner and outer, or of understanding how this inner transformation would take place except through transcendent means.

For Parfitt (2002), writing from a skeptically critical position, the best that post modernism can offer is an ethics of "least violence", since violence is never far away in the encounter between the self and other. The very nature of deconstructionism, with its openness to alterity, leaves it prepared for working against the worst excesses of the inevitable violence that occurs when making judgments in the relationship between self and others.

From an anthropological perspective, Quarles Van Ufford and Giri (2003) set out a more nuanced understanding of the moral relationship between self and other in the development context, and a clearer explanation of their interdependence. Referring to Schrag (1997) the authors point to the need for us to be familiar with the "grammar of paradox", balancing the need for the care of the self with the care for others, as well as the particularity of the exchange. The authors also draw on Alasdair MacIntyre to:

Help us understand the qualities that are required to participate in a relationship which involves not only an abstract self and an abstract other, but also a particular self and a particular other, or particular selves and particular others. For MacIntyre neither the language of self-interest nor the language of benevolence is enough. Instead it needs a language of giving and receiving in which both the self and the other are giver and receiver at the same time ... This mode of engagement ... urges us to be attentive to how interdependence is put into place in the practice of development, for example the dialectic between goal and result, the interaction between actors and target groups, others and self.

(Quarles Van Ufford and Giri, 2003: 272–3)

Although acknowledging interdependence, the balancing of ethics and esthetics, the authors also aspire to a "transcendent inspiration of unconditional love" to put development back on a more moral footing. The anthropological journey takes us a long way away from the individual and helps us begin to understand the dynamic nature of human inter-relating, but also strays into slightly naive transcendentalism. Whilst drawing attention to the need for a greater understanding of paradox, the authors manage to diffuse some of the more radical implications of enduring a paradox into an almost classical incremental action-reflection model aiming at balance. What is significant here is that Giri and Quarles Van Ufford seem to be ignoring the paradox at the heart of what MacIntyre is saying where development practitioners are givers and receivers *at the same time*. This is not simply a question of balance, but a relationship of opposites in tension always negating each other. In this sense I would argue that they have yet to acquire "the grammar of paradox" to which they point, rendering it rather into an attempt to acknowledge the two aspects, giver and receiver, in the same account as two separate phases. In this there is no dialectic, no dynamism.

I have made the case above that the instrumentalist understanding of power relating at the individual level is weak, and I gave one example where one of the main writers in the instrumental tradition gave a prescription for the discovery of our "inner selves" as a means of putting the relationship between self and others on a different footing. For the post-modernists, the triumph of one side over another is inevitable but can be mitigated with a doctrine of "least harm". The social anthropological school enjoins a paradoxical understanding of the relationship between self and others but ultimately tries to resolve the paradox with a reflective incrementalism and an injunction toward balance or homeostasis. In this respect their preferred paradigm seems to be open systems theory where they assume the ideal state to be one of homeostasis.

I doubt that any other field of practice has managed to sustain such a strong set of ideals which are so clearly utopian as that of international development. I hope that I have demonstrated above that the international development literature is exceptionally theory-rich and is populated by people who are keen to measure what they do against "significant horizons". My reflections on my own practice in the development context, however, have led me to feel that none of the theories explored above have offered me sufficient explanation of what has happened to me during a career in development. In my experience, NGOs were often filled with high-minded but sometimes impractical people who tended toward utopianism, amongst whom I would include myself; managerialism seemed to offer a way out of the ideological impasse so that we could spend less time talking about politics and more time getting the work done. However, subsequently I have experienced managerialism as driving out issues of politics and power to such an extent that ways of working appear to me to be completely inconsistent with the values base of what development organizations are set up to do, and in contradiction with my own values too. The political in the context of development seems to have become a landscape of human undertaking virtually indistinguishable from any other, such as enterprise or banking.

Next I will explore below how the theory of complex responsive processes understands power relating and the interaction between self and others. I will do so because I understand this to be offering a much more radically social understanding of power relating as well as a much more dynamic and generative concept of paradox at the center of the creation and recreation of values. I will explore the theory of complex responsive processes as a foil to the theories considered above because it seems to me to be offering an understanding of the way that humans interrelate that is based neither in metaphysics, nor in an open systems conception of the balancing of needs and priorities as homeostasis, nor yet in a primeval and violent struggle between one narrative and another. It does indeed share some of the criticisms of instrumentalism voiced both by the social anthropologists and the post-modernists, but it also differs in significant ways from them and this is what I hope to explore below.

Complex responsive processes – recognition of the self through others

I will turn to this theory (Stacey, 2000; Stacey *et al.*, 2000; Griffin, 2002) to see what it might add to the ideas set out above as a way of understanding my experience in country B and the exploration of values and power relating that we have begun to disentangle above. Where the proponents of complex responsive processes would appear to me to radically part company with both the post-modernists and the social anthropological approach outlined above, is in their understanding of the dynamics of communicating and power-relating, and the radical paradoxes that these involve, and how this affects the creation and recreation of values. The theory of complex responsive processes understands organizations as the complex patterning of repeated non-linear interactions between human bodies. Because humans are involved feelings are always aroused as are three inter-related aspects of relating, which are communicative interaction, power relating and the evaluative choices people make. Drawing on the work of Elias (e.g. 1978) and Mead (e.g. 1934), the theory understands power as a necessary expression of human relations because we are inter-dependent. Elias uses different analogies to explain his understanding of power relating, and has variously described it as being like a dance (1968) or like a game of chess (1978). When two people play chess together they each need the other to play the game – each serves a function for the other, and the moves of one player inform the moves of the other. It would be difficult to understand the sense of a player's move out of the context of his or her opponent's moves:

> Like the concept of power, the concept of function must be understood as a concept of relationship ... when one person (or group of persons) lacks something which another person or group has the power to withhold, the latter has a function for the former ... people or groups that have functions for each other exercise constraints over each other.
>
> (Elias, 1978: 78)

Elias' understanding of power relating introduces the notions of interdependence and yet can still entertain the idea of power imbalances, as one side, with greater ability or knowledge, can dictate the course of play more than the other. This is a very different understanding of power relating than that demonstrated by the post-modernists, where power and violence are interlinked, and the social anthropological school which seems to be striving for some kind of power balance. In some senses, for Elias, even in a situation of imbalance, the more powerful still needs the less powerful; each constrains the other in the figuration of relationship, but that is not to say that their freedom for action or their moral responsibility toward each other is equal. The term "figuration" is at the heart of Elias' work and by it he meant the structural interdependence between humans that describes all relationships.

But when the power of two chess opponents is equivalent then they both have less chance of manipulating each other, thus producing a game that neither of them has planned. This is the kind of relating that Elias (1974) thought most closely resembled the social process, where each of us interacts with our own intentions, desires and values, but where the outcome emerges in the interplay of these and so cannot be predicted. And in the NGO B and Donor A example, with the help of Elias, one can see that they do have a clear function for each other. Donor A needs NGO B for its local links and expertise in project managing water and sanitation projects. Equally, NGO B needs the status and cash that a relationship with Donor A can provide. In the departure of one set of Donor A staff and the arrival of another, along with the change in country representative for NGO B, power tipped toward Donor A in their attempts to impose a particular way of doing the work on NGO B. I want to go on to argue that what is also taking place is a struggle, like a chess game, over different value systems. What Donor A has the power to withhold, in the words of the quotation above, is the ability not to acknowledge the existing sets of relationships between NGO B and the organizations it calls its partners. In so doing, I will have to unpack further the process of human relating described by Mead and attempt to explain why this is so critical to the understanding of the relationship between power and values.

Mead (1934) builds a theory of human communicative interaction which suggests that humans are capable of gesturing or communicating with others in ways that draw forth the same range of responses in themselves as they draw forth from others. This is how we might intuit how another person might react to the way we are communicating with them. Mead went on to argue that humans are essentially role-playing animals and that is was possible for the body to call forth responses in itself. Just as humans can gesture to others and call forth a response, so it is possible for someone to do the same to themselves, and it is this private role playing of gestures that constitutes mind. Mead argued that this capacity to have a conversation of gestures with oneself, evolves over time until we are able to take the attitude of many others in a generalized way. Humans engaged in this conversation of gestures can take the attitude of the "generalized other". We are able to take the social attitude into account as we gesture and respond. More than this Mead argues that we are able to take the attitude of a generalized other to ourselves.

Because we are able to be an object to ourselves we are capable of responding as an "I" to the generalized responses of others as a "me": "The 'I' is the response of the organism to the attitudes of the others, the 'me' is the organized set of attitudes of others which one himself assumes" (Mead, 1934: 175).

Mead argues that this is how the self arises, in the dialectic between the spontaneous "I" and the "me" that arises out of a symbolically generalized sense of others' perspectives, which are taken up in one's relating to oneself. Two other things are important in Mead's theory. The first is that he did not think that there was a predetermined way that the "I" might respond to the "me" – the outcome is always potentially unpredictable. There is always a choice and the potential for spontaneity. The other is that this juxtaposition of the "I" and the "me" cannot be thought of as happening in separate phases. They both arise together and together constitute the self. Human interaction, then, is a continuous process of gesture and response, the actions and feelings of bodies, including the bodily action of language. We are continuously calling forth responses in ourselves and in others which in turn informs the next response from ourselves and from them; in this process what we call mind and self are arising simultaneously.

Rights and solidarity

Honneth (1995), building on the ideas of Hegel and Mead concerning the inter-subjectively formed self, presents a social anthropological theory of mutual recognition as the basis for a moral theory. He argues that these processes arise as self-confidence based on love, self-respect based on rights and self-esteem based on solidarity. Honneth contends that:

> The reproduction of social life is governed by the imperative for mutual recognition, because one can develop a practical relation-to-self only when one has learned to view oneself, from the normative perspective of one's partners in interaction, as their social addressee.
>
> (Honneth, 1995: 93)

Rights and solidarity are two terms which are very important in the international development arena and I believe that Honneth can help to uncover a different way of thinking about them. My area of interest is in the fact that I am coming to believe that NGO B's frustration with the Donor A, and the partners' frustration with both NGO B and Donor A, is partly based on the feeling of not being recognized in the way that they see themselves, and on the fact that the recognition between the parties takes different forms. In essence I think the relationship between Donor A and NGO B is prioritized on legal recognition and calls forth rights and duties, and the relationship between NGO B and its partners is prioritized on the solidarity that emanates from shared values, and this is what NGO B has come to mean in the term "partnership". I would go further and want to argue that certain ways of working in organizations and the belief systems that they embody make it harder for individual staff members, such as the one I encountered, to recognize themselves and their values in the way that they have to work.

In terms of legal recognition, Honneth develops Hegel and Mead's theory of the generalized other to state that it describes "the situation in which self and other respect each other as legal subjects for the sole reason that they are aware of the social norms by which rights and duties are distributed in their community" (Honneth, 1995: 109). Formalized legal rights and duties are the result of a long historical process of struggle and can be traced back to the very process of "I-me" dialectic outlined above. Honneth shows how the decoupling of legal rights from issues of status has brought about a continued dynamic to expand the context of rights:

> The cumulative expansion of rights-claims, which is what we are dealing with in modern societies, can be understood as a process in which the scope of the general features of a moral responsible person has gradually increased, because, under pressure from struggles for recognition, ever-new prerequisites for participation in rational will-formation have to be taken into consideration.
>
> (Honneth, 1995: 115)

Honneth demonstrates the contexts in which the struggle for recognition may arise, in situations where universal moral principles have been enshrined in law and are challenged by groups who find themselves excluded from that universalized description. He nonetheless also points out that paradoxically, by their very universalist nature, the characteristics of legally enshrined rights that make them challengeable are that exceptions and privileges are no longer admissible. In this sense Honneth has pointed to a true and irresolvable paradox that creates movement of thought. So, for example, in the relationship between Donor A and NGO B, defined as a legal contract, there is an assumption that there is an agreement between parties on rationally agreed norms; the contingent exceptions of context, culture, ways of working, are currently not being viewed as admissible reasons for failure to adhere to the contract as specified. In signing this contract NGO B has aspired to be a fully recognized citizen with all the respect that will accompany this recognition within the community of development agencies and donors, but it is a community with a particular set of values and assumptions about the way that development can work. The paradox for NGO B is that the relationships of solidarity it has built up with its partners are negated by the very contract that it has signed, which recognizes only standardized development outputs, or "deliverables".

Honneth contrasts legal recognition with a third form of recognition, solidarity, which I think more closely mirrors the kind of relationship that NGO B believes that it has with its partners:

Unlike modern legal recognition, social esteem is directed, as we have seen, at the particular qualities that characterize people in their personal difference. Thus, whereas modern law represents a medium of recognition that represents the universal features of human subjects, this form of recognition demands a social medium that must be able to express the characteristic differences among human subjects in a universal and, more specifically intersubjectively obligatory way.... This form of mutual recognition is thus also tied to the presupposition of a context of social life whose members, through their orientation towards shared conceptions of their goals, form a community of value.

(Honneth, 1995: 122)

He argues that the relationship of solidarity presupposes a kind of symmetry or equivalence between the two parties who share the same feeling; that each is trying to accomplish something of worth that is valued by the other. In thinking about country B and the contractual relationship between Donor A and NGO B, and NGO B and its partners, it might be possible to describe them along a number of axes of recognition. Donor A recognizes NGO B as a rational partner in a mutually agreed undertaking, freely consented to, to scale up their area of activity and to deliver to punishing targets. NGO B is recognized as a full legal partner. In contradistinction, what links NGO B and the partners, in their own terms, is the shared value horizons, the mutual recognition of solidarity, which is as much to do with the way that work gets accomplished as what the work is. Donor A is pressuring NGO B to work with the partners in the way that it is trying to work with NGO B, at a distance from the exceptions and contingencies that threaten to challenge instrumentalism. An interesting conflict arises as these two separate prioritizations get mediated in the day to day, and in general Donor A takes itself out of the fray by being too busy, by employing consultants like me or by working through NGO B. NGO B has still not yet learnt to find a voice to argue for its own perspective in the relationship, to expand the Donor A's horizons of what is and is not "reasonable", in the words of the Donor A staff member.

The instrumentalist paradigm within which Donor A operates, idealizes planning and control and suggests that, when "problems" occur, the way to "solve" them is to exert more control and introduce more planning and policy papers. There is often little thought about the contingent nature of what is happening since managerialism resorts to what is known as "best practice", that is to say, tried and tested methods from elsewhere which are guaranteed to work. So, for example, anxiety on the part of the Donor A staff member at the lack of progress led her to exert more and more pressure on the staff in NGO B to perform as they were expected, which in turn led to them wanting to "speed up" the project by recruiting more partners, bogging them down in even more preparatory work before they could start implementing. The anxiety at the delay also led the Donor A staff member to behave in ways which, even from my brief experience of her, I feel she would consider unacceptable, which she began to admit herself when I offered her the opportunity to reflect upon the situation she found herself in. This made working relationships difficult between Donor A and NGO B, as well as between NGO B and the organizations it calls partners and began to call into question the very values that the project was set up to embody – "empowerment", equity and partnership. Rather than question the assumptions upon which the plan was based Donor A employees would choose to question the competence and professionalism of the people they had contracted to do the work. In turn staff in NGO B in country B had begun to question the nature of their own relationships with organizations they term partners and began to unravel the relationship of solidarity that they have had over many years.

Conclusions

In my consultancy in Country B I experienced in a practical way how value positions inevitably come into conflict in the undertaking of development work and are mediated by relationships of power. In taking up the Elias' deliberations on power and Mead's theories of the emergence of self, which are two cornerstones of the theories of complex responsive processes of relating, I have used them as a basis for contrasting with other theories currently in use which attempt to explain some of the dynamics of international development. I have also pursued Honneth as he takes up Mead's theories as a way of trying to understand the creation of values in the context of every day human interaction that I described in the narrative. My conclusion is that Honneth's development of Mead's theories is useful, and the concept of mutual recognition is helpful, but has yet to fully capture the paradox in the "I-me" dialectic or the paradoxical interrelation of individuals and society as described by Elias.

References

Ankersmit, F. (1996) *Aesthetic Politics: Political Philosophy beyond Fact and Value*, Stanford: Stanford University Press.

Bruner, J. (1986) *Actual Meanings, Possible Worlds*, Cambridge, MA: Harvard University Press.

Burkitt, I. (1999) *Bodies of Thought: Embodiment, Identity and Modernity*, London: Sage.

Chambers, R. (1997) *Whose Reality Counts?: Putting the First Last*, Rugby: ITDG Publications.

Chambers, R. (2002) *Participatory Workshops: A Sourcebook of 21 Sets of Ideas and Activities*, London: Earthscan.

Cleaver, F. (2002) "Paradoxes of participation: Questioning participatory approaches to development", in Edwards, E. and Fowler, A. (eds.) *The Earthscan Reader on NGO Management*, London: Earthscan.

Cooke, B. and Kothari, U. (eds.) (2001) *Participation the New Tyranny?*, London: Zed Books.

Cowen, M. P. and Shenton, R. W. (1996) *Doctrines of Development*, London: Routledge.

Dewey, J. (1934) *A Common Faith*, New Haven, Conn: Yale University Press.

Edwards, M. and Hulme, D. (eds.) (1992) *Making a Difference: NGOs and Development in a Changing World*, London: Earthscan.

Edwards, M. and Hulme, D. (eds.) (1992) *Non-governmental Organizations: Performance and Accountability*, London: Earthscan.

Edwards, E. and Sen, G. (2002) "NGOs, social change and the transformation of human relationships: A 21st century civic agenda", in Edwards, E. and Fowler, A. (eds.) *The Earthscan Reader on NGO Management*, London: Earthscan.

Elias, N. (1968) *The History of Manners*, New York: Pantheon Books.

Elias, N. (1974) *The Civilizing Process*, Oxford: Blackwell.

Elias, N. (1978) *What is Sociology?*, New York: Columbia University Press.

Escobar, A. (1995) *Encountering Development: The Making and Unmaking of the Third World*, Princeton, NJ: Princeton University Press.

Esteva, G. and Prakash, M. S. (1998) "Beyond development, what?", *Development in Practice*, 8: 3–9.

Eyben, R. (2003) "Donors as political actors: Fighting the Thirty Years War in Bolivia", *IDS Working Paper no. 183*, Brighton: Institute of Development Studies.

Foucault, M. (1984) "Truth and power" in Rabinow, P. (ed.) *The Foucault Reader: An Introduction to Foucault's Thought*, London: Penguin.

Fowler, A. (1997) *Striking a Balance: A Guide to Enhancing the Effectiveness of Non-governmental Organizations in International Development*, London: Earthscan.

Fowler, A. (2000) *The Virtuous Spiral: A Guide to Sustainability for NGOs in International Development*, London: Earthscan.

Griffin, D. (2002) *The Emergence of Leadership: Linking Self-organization and Ethics*, London: Routledge.

Honneth, A. (1995) *The Struggle for Recognition*, Oxford: Polity.

Joas, H. (2000) *The Genesis of Values*, Cambridge: Polity.

MacIntyre, A. (1999) *Dependent Rational Animals*, London: Duckworth.

Mead, G. H. (1914) "The psychological bases of internationalism", *Survey*, 23: 604–7.

Mead, G. H. (1932) "Scientific method and the moral sciences", *International Journal of Ethics*, 33: 229–47.

Mead, G. H. (1934) *Mind, Self and Society: From the Standpoint of a Social Behaviorist*, Chicago: University of Chicago Press.

Mosse, D. (2005) *Cultivating Development: An Ethnography of Aid Policy and Practice*, London: Pluto.

Parfitt, T. (2002) *The End of Development: Modernity, Post-modernity and Development*, London: Pluto.

Quarles Van Ufford, P. and Giri, K. G. (eds.) (2003) *A Moral Critique of Development: In Search of Global Responsibilities*, London: Routledge.

Schrag, C. O. (1997) *The Self After Post-modernity*, Princeton: Princeton University Press.

Shaw, P. (2002) *Changing Conversations in Organizations: A Complexity Approach to Change*, London: Routledge.

Stacey, R., Griffin, D. and Shaw, P. (2000) *Complexity and Management: Fad or Radical Challenge to Systems Thinking?*, London: Routledge.

Stacey, R. and Griffin, D. (eds.) (2005) *A Complexity Perspective on Researching Organizations: Taking Experience Seriously*, London: Routledge.

Stacey, R. (2000) *Strategic Management and Organizational Dynamics: The Challenge of Complexity*, London: Pearson.

Taylor, C. (1991) *The Ethics Of Authenticity*, Cambridge: Harvard University Press.

Editors' introduction to Chapter 3

At the time of writing this chapter, Arnie Grant was the managing director of a division of a large services company. He was appointed to lead the negotiation of a major new labor contract with the Unions for the whole group of companies. The story of these negotiations provides an opportunity to reflect upon the nature of conflict, not just in labor contract negotiations, but in organizational life in general. Grant was acutely aware of how the previous contract had been agreed with Unions in 1999 but, despite Union agreement, had failed to command the support of Union members who subsequently called for unofficial strike action. He was anxious to avoid a repeat of such damaging strike actions and was also concerned that any new agreement should preserve enough flexibility to deal with the changes in work practices that would be entailed in the strategic move to a new distribution system. He was, therefore, sensitive to the enormous potential for damaging conflict during and after the negotiation process. Against this background he decided to adopt a somewhat unusual approach to the negotiations in holding off taking a clear negotiating position as long as he could. In late 2003, he took responsibility for the negotiations which were supposed to produce a new contract to run from the start of 2005. He spent well over a year creating opportunities for discussion and relationship building, even to the point of delaying the actual negotiations past the scheduled starting date for the new agreement, and it was only in March 2005 that the negotiations proper took place, producing a widely supported new agreement in that same month.

In making sense of what he was doing, Grant explored the literature on conflict in both sociology and organizational theory. In this chapter, he describes how much of that literature understands conflict as a characteristic of antagonistic relationships between people. These writers tend to categorize such antagonistic conflict into different types such as instrumental, realistic or substantive conflict generated by different views of means and ends in addressing a problem, on the one hand, and social, power, dependency, unrealistic and emotional conflict generated by different personal agendas and feelings, on the other. Different prescriptions are then provided for dealing with these different types of conflict, often accompanied by a warning against avoiding or suppressing conflict because this can then lead conflict to surface in unexpected forms. The aim of the prescriptions is to produce consensus and solve problems. Grant contrasts this way of thinking about conflict with that to be found in the theory of complex responsive processes which draws on the views of Elias and Mead. Here, conflict is not understood simply in antagonist terms but is regarded as an inevitable aspect of all human relationships arising from the need to interpret generalized norms and idealized values in particular contingent situations and from the fact that human interdependence means that all human relationships are power relationships.

This leads Grant to draw a distinction between what he calls polarized conflict, in which people take up fixed win–lose positions, and explorative conflict, in which they carry on talking about their differences and negotiating a way of going on together. He does not, however, see these as distinct types of human conflict, but as aspects of human relating that are never far from each other. Purposefully engaging others in explorative conflict does indeed "open up a can of worms", requiring leaders and managers to accept not being in control and take the risk that issues will emerge which they may find difficult to deal with. In other words, it requires leaders and managers to recognize that polarized conflict can very easily emerge in the course of explorative conflict, producing surprises that those involved will find themselves having to deal with if they are to avoid getting "stuck". However, the alternative of keeping the "can of worms" tightly shut also runs the risk of polarized conflict emerging in what then becomes very "stuck". Grant also makes it clear that he is not offering his experience as some kind of "best practice" prescription for successful conflict management. Although the story is one of a successful negotiation, he stresses his inability to control all the factors involved and the inevitable surprises that occurred along the way. So, although there is a successful outcome to the negotiation, events elsewhere, over which he and his colleagues have no control, still lead to a strike.

In following this story, it is no surprise that conflict between company executives and union officials is an ever-present possibility. Interestingly, however, the story brings out the conflicts that occur between the executives of the company as they take different positions on the possibility of offering job security in return for job flexibility. This too produces surprises.

Grant makes another important point. He describes how the population-wide patterns of interaction between people, which is what we can understand organizational strategy to be, emerges in the many, many local interactions between people and groupings of people.

So while, in Chapter 2, Mowles draws our attention to the nature of values and ideology as the basis for conflict, this chapter focuses our attention on the nature of conflict in the ordinary everyday lives of people in organizations.

3 Working at the edge of polarized conflict in organizations

Arnie Grant

This chapter describes an 18 month period in which I led the team negotiating a labor agreement for a large group of services companies (25,000) employees. I explore the formation of the negotiation team, internal relations within the team and relations with union leaders, managers, and board members, as well as the politics and other developments that led to the final agreement. The narrative explores the way in which global patterns of interaction continuously emerged in local interactions as I experimented with approaches to leadership with the intention of securing acceptable results. Conflict, or in some cases the avoidance of conflict, played an important role in organizational life, including the negotiation of a labor agreement. I consider how conflict might be thought about, how it is explained by different authors, how it connects to negotiation processes and how global patterns emerge in the local interactions of negotiation. I make a link to the unpredictability of strategic processes and the effect this has on the negotiations.

As a member of the Executive Board (EXB), I was responsible as managing director for one of the Specialized Divisions. I joined this organization after it had experienced a period of upheaval. The source of the upheaval was a conflict in 1999 between the directors, the unions, Staff Councils and the majority of the staff running operations, about a plan for organizational change regarding employee work patterns. A binding agreement had been entered into with the unions so that, even though they were unable to convince their members to accept these changes, they had no choice but to continue their support for the new patterns. Union and non-union members slowly but surely started to form sub-groups. Short strikes were initiated by these groups which seriously affected production.

As a result of this emerging conflict and its breakdown consequences, some new directors were appointed and in 2002 a recovery period started. Six new labor agreements were finalized for divisions and departments covering the period January 1, 2003 to December 31, 2004. Headquarter staff were included in the General Services Division agreement which meant that it covered 12,000 of the company's 25,000 employees, making it by far the most important of the six separate labor agreements covering the whole company. After a remarkable improvement over the past few years, our company now faces new challenges.

New electronic distribution systems (EDS) will be introduced. This will have a major impact on organizational and strategic developments, particularly changes in work practices for almost all of the 12,000 operational staff members working in this area. The Staff Councils participated in the decision making process around the new distribution system but it was clear that the new labor agreement to replace the one expiring at the end of 2004 would also have an impact. As one of the leaders I realized that there is always the potential for conflict during such strategic change and I was anxious to avoid a repetition of the 2001 strike.

The Director of Human Resource Management in the General Services Division, a former union leader, had led the most important negotiation team for the agreement that was to expire at the end of 2004. He had introduced some new items during these negotiations, such as Job Security for a part of the operational staff in exchange for Flexibility (JSF). In late 2003, this Director changed careers and the HRM manager of the Group left, while a new HRM director was yet to be appointed. At the same time a new policy was adopted to bring all divisions closer together in the light of possible future developments, meaning going from six labor agreements to one for the whole company. The Board decided to ask one of the managing directors to lead the forthcoming negotiations on behalf of the whole Group. In December 2003, the CEO of the Group asked me whether I would be willing to lead the negotiations with the unions regarding a new labor agreement for the period starting on the 1st of January 2005. I agreed. From the moment the request was made I started to think about how this agreement could play a role in our future strategic change program on the introduction of EDS. Major changes were laying ahead and a good agreement could facilitate these changes. One thing I focused on was to secure this agreement in a responsible way without the polarized labor conflict which had led to the breakdown in 2001, putting our reputation in jeopardy.

What I have discovered in working for our company is that there is a gap between top management and people in operations, on the one hand, and planning and execution, on the other. This, in combination with a lack of trust and superficial relations between these groups, always creates a basis for polarized conflict. During the past years, the unions have tended to refer to company management as "those stupid idiots up there who do not know what they are talking about. We will stand up for the workers to see that no wrong is done". Both, of course, are not true but it was the way it was presented. This way of thinking created an advantageous position from the union point of view. Many times even small organizational changes led to conflict. So, trying to avoid polarized conflict means, among other things, building better relations which require an investment of time and energy in engaging people and taking them seriously concerning the work they do. This intention of doing what was required to avoid polarized conflict without weakening our negotiation position, very much influenced the thinking during the whole negotiation process. Focusing on preventing polarized conflict by building good relationships is not generally the starting position in most negotiations but it provides an opportunity to look at negotiations from another angle.

Reflection on the overriding intention of avoiding polarized conflict

From the start I had a clear overall intention of avoiding conflict by focusing, not on a negotiating position, but on building relationships in order to avoid this situation. Reflecting on this overriding intention, in writing this chapter, I am not only exploring the nature and role of conflict in terms of this particular labor agreement negotiation but generally in organizational life. We, the company, discovered that we were not able to handle the previous conflict in a way that served the purpose of an acceptable outcome. Also based on the fact that we did not know how relations with the unions and the opinion leaders in our workforce developed during the last years, we were not sure how any conflict would present itself during these negotiations. In reflecting on what happened during the negotiation period I have come to see the importance of distinguishing between different meanings and forms of conflict in literature and practice.

A typical definition of conflict describes it as a social phenomenon involving a struggle aimed at neutralizing, injuring or eliminating the values, status, power and resources of opponents (Coser, 1956; Rapoport, 1974; Glasl, 1999). Conflict, then, has the meaning of a relationship between foes characterized by hostility, fight and even breakdown in cooperation. One could speak in this case of *"polarized conflict"*. Writers in this tradition tend to say little about how conflict emerges and focus instead on how to prevent (Mastenbroek, 1996; Schermerhorn *et al.*, 1991) or "solve" conflict, involving the ability to handle misunderstanding and tension in organizations. Some warn against suppressing conflictual feelings, because this could surface as other polarized forms of conflict, and advocate instead the bringing of differences into the open (Glasl, 1999). One could call this *"preventive or repressive conflict"*.

Writers also typically classify conflict into different categories, proposing different interventions to deal with different types of conflict. Mastenbroek (1996), for example, identifies: instrumental conflicts about priorities, resulting from insufficient communication and unclear division of responsibilities; social, emotional conflicts relating to personal relationships, trust and self-image; negotiation conflicts arising in the tension around sharing scarce goods; and power/dependency questions reflected in rivalry about position. Schermerhorn *et al.* (1991) distinguish between *substantitive conflicts* which are disagreements over ends and means, such as the allocation of resources, distribution of rewards, policies and procedures, and *emotional conflicts* which involve feelings of anger, mistrust, dislike, fear, resentment and personal clashes. Although it is difficult to separate them, Schermerhorn *et al.* argue that each form must be dealt with each on its own merits. Schermerhorn *et al.* (1991) also make the following distinctions: role conflict which occurs when people are unable to respond to the standards of one or more members of the group they normally work with; intrapersonal conflict; interpersonal conflict; inter-group conflict; and inter-organizational conflict. Schermerhorn *et al.* focus on the ability of the manager to encounter and deal with each level of conflict, specifically from the organizational standpoint. They hold that conflict resolution can only be achieved when the underlying reasons for conflicts are eliminated and propose several management techniques to help the manager to solve the problem.

The question might be asked whether prevention of conflict in this way will lead to desired developments in organizations. When conflict occurs, solutions also provide the opportunities to implement necessary change in an organization, implying that conflict is not always a bad thing. Taking another view, Mead (1934), Elias (1978) and Griffin (2002), see conflict as a normal result of people interacting to reach an acceptable next step in discussing goals. This can be called *"natural or normative conflict"*. Normative from this perspective is used to describe the effect of those structures of culture which regulate the function of social activity. Conflict can be seen as an ongoing process of discussing and exploring difference, involving both cooperation and competition without necessarily breaking down as hostility of some kind. In this case you could see conflict as a description of relationships. This is a relationship of exploration, as opposed to the relationship of confrontation stressed by the writers mentioned above. This can be called *"explorative conflict"*.

Griffin (2002) introduces conflict as an aspect of the emergence of leadership, in focusing on the difference between cult leadership and functional leadership. Cult values such as cult leadership are the idealization of standards of the world or the organization in which one lives and works. For example, the cult value is that all services should be delivered on time, where the reality is that all kinds of influences on a services system result in an acceptable percentage of punctual deliveries. This is the functionalization of the standards and makes them real in day to day practice. Cult leadership shows the same phenomenon. Every performance has to match maximum standards, where reality shows that this will not be the case. The discussion between managers, leaders and the people they work with will lead to the recognition of diverse opinions and this recognition will take place through conflict, in which case conflict is a very normal part of our day to day responsibilities. Good examples can be found in every election campaign where presenting an ideal reality is not good enough to get elected. After the election the politician has to transfer (functionalize) his ideals into usable plans for the time to come, in interaction with his voters and parliament. Griffin also points out that "conflict" itself can be idealized by removing it from the present and making it hypothetical; just pretend that it does not exist and it becomes a cult value. Not talking about the possibility that conflict can emerge when choices between two conflicting proposals are to be made is in itself seen by Griffin as cult leadership, an idealization.

In taking the above view, Griffin refers to Mead who sees conflict as the very core of his theory of ethics and leadership and states that it is through conflict that we are continuously recreating our world and becoming ourselves, that is, our identity.

> Human individuals realize or become aware of themselves as such, almost more easily and readily in terms of the social attitudes connected or

associated with these two "hostile" impulses, *self protection and self preservation* (or in terms of these two impulses as expressed in these attitudes) than they do in terms of any other social attitudes or behavior tendencies as expressed by those attitudes.

(Mead, 1934: 304)

Griffin also refers to the importance of conflict as seen by N. Elias: "One of the most astonishing features of many sociological and economical theories is that they scarcely acknowledge the central part played in every social development by tension and conflicts" (Elias, 1978: 172).

Griffin does not see conflict as something threatening or as something you should avoid, but as a normal result of interaction between people and an integral part of leadership. Ordinary life is an ongoing exploration and negotiation of conflicting positions and this need not be immediately polarized. Such ordinary conflict cannot be managed away or resolved.

By now it is clear that there is not something universal called conflict. It is important to try to prevent polarized conflict and to avoid the repressed conflict that could so easily become polarized, but explorative conflict, as part of the continuous process of relating can create solutions and prevent people from getting stuck. The position Griffin, Mead and Elias take is reflected in the theory of complex responsive processes (Griffin, 2002). With regards to the negotiation process I was about to engage in, the explorative conflict involved in building up relations with the union people was to become important. Building up relations means that parties have to engage without moving into a polarized conflict situation. Working with explorative conflict always holds the risk of entering polarized conflict. My experience is that there is only a thin line separating these two areas. When I started investigating conflict I saw it as a general way of describing people disagreeing about opinions and views. In the course of reflecting and writing, I have come to see the question of conflict in a more complex way, although at the time of the negotiations my understanding and actions were much more intuitive. In the following sections, I will describe how the process of relating has evolved. I will also present an argument which links conflict to identity, ideology and how to work in an explorative way at the edge of polarized conflict in negotiating a sensitive labor contract.

Preparing for the negotiation of a new unified labor agreement

Returning to early 2004, I want now to describe some of the preparations we made for the negotiations with the unions. Three main groups were involved: the nine members of the Company Executive Board (EXB); the four Union Leaders who act as a group when negotiating but are competing when representing their own members; and the six members of the Negotiating Team. After several consultations with the chairman of the EXB, I presented the first steps of a possible future strategic change program to the EXB on February 16. These included proposals for job security and staff reduction. I followed the business plan of the General Services Division and tried to combine this with the plans of the other Specialized Divisions. Shortly after this presentation I was invited by the 11 HRM managers of all divisions and subsidiary companies to share my first impressions. I gave them the same EXB overview and sensed a strong fear of being excluded from the process as a group. Labor agreements were always part of the domain of the HRM people and now somebody else had taken over. I understood their feelings, but it was not yet the time to include this large group in my work in progress, as I was concerned that they would strongly push to continue business as usual and I wanted to be free to make up my mind on how to move things forward. I planned conversations with many other colleagues who, in one way or another, play an important part in how the company is managed and who would have to live with the outcome of our negotiations.

During a financial information meeting at the end of February, I was introduced to the Union Leaders, Boris, Charles, Karl and Stef, as the negotiator for a new combined company labor agreement. These meetings have something of a cat and mouse game, in which the company is the cat and the union representatives are the mice.

Next, I had to form the negotiating team. From the beginning I was looking for an emergent way to get the negotiating process started rather than making clear, fixed decisions right at the start about what we needed to achieve and how we should go about achieving it. I was in no hurry because the government was proposing major changes in many social systems, including pensions, which would feature in our negotiations. In early 2004 it was very unclear just what the changes would be and so I wanted to go as slowly as possible toward the actual negotiation with the unions. I was also very aware of the events of 1999 when the unions had not been able to persuade their own members. It was important, therefore, to invite onto the negotiating team people with expert knowledge, and/or enough support from the managers in the division they represented, to take up the responsibility for negotiating together with me and feel comfortable in working together in an emergent way. The internal political forces and pressures always increase during the process and I was reluctant to let these forces influence our work too early and in a way that would make it difficult for us to hold on to our own emergent thinking. One thing was certain, one day there would be a new labor agreement but the rest was open for discussion. So, I had talks with each of the candidates for the negotiating team individually, sharing my views on the way I would like to work together. For some it was a little unusual not to sit down, think it over and present a point of view on how to move forward and what to get out of the process. Everybody was asked whether they were comfortable with working together in this emergent way. In March 2004, I presented the first draft on the team composition at the EXB meeting.

March 29, 2004 was a big day. We had our first meeting of the negotiating team and introduced ourselves to each other. We decided to meet every two weeks in the afternoon on the day of the EXB meeting to talk about whatever was going on. Our biggest friend was time and we wanted to keep it that way.

We started our first meeting just talking. Since our future as a team and what we might achieve together was uncertain, we wanted to give ourselves enough room to maneuver without putting all kinds of constraints on ourselves. Our own day-to-day experience gave us enough food for talk and thought to connect to the process at hand. In one of her examples, Shaw describes how one of her clients wants to encourage his people to open up and accept new turbulence. She describes her feelings as follows.

> At this point I talk about my interest in the concept of "edge of chaos" conditions in which a complex network paradoxically experiences both stability and instability – where variations in the reproduction of existing patterns may amplify to generate real novelty. I talk about how such self-organizing emergence is intrinsically uncontrollable in the usual sense and unpredictable in the longer term. I said that I was interested in working with the self organizing processes far from certainty and agreement where people really did not and could not know precisely what they were doing as they acted into an evolving situation.
>
> (Shaw, 2002: 93)

Working with a team that was partly selected by me and partly selected itself, it was possible to exchange ideas and start feeling comfortable in not knowing. We were very clear about the fact that we needed to build up informal relations with the union leaders. Godfried, a member of the team who came from the General Services Division as a labor relations expert, had built up such relations over the past few years and this created the kind of starting position we wanted to be in. It surely would help to prevent polarized conflict from emerging and facilitate dealing with the more normal exploratory conflict situations which come up in every discussion (Mead, 1934). During the final stages of the negotiations, Godfried and I had many opportunities to make use of these good relations in discussing subjects on an individual basis outside the conference room, which is often the case during complicated negotiations (Mastenbroek, 1994). During almost every negotiation team meeting we talked about major developments in government policies on subjects connected to our negotiations. Step by step our knowledge base increased and we felt more comfortable about widening the circle of people we would like to involve in the discussions.

The first union leader I met on an individual basis was Karl from one of the largest unions. He warned me about the attitude of one of the other unions which was intent on destabilization. I thanked him for his concern, but as always with warnings; most of the time I had no idea what to do with them. Boris, another union leader, had a clear view of what he wanted to talk about and was well prepared. In fact he came up with many of the subjects we had identified ourselves. Boris was also partly responsible for the agreements with the government department providing the logistic infrastructure and was worried about the way their negotiation process was developing. The government is still responsible for much of the logistic infrastructure. In the early days it had been one entity but it had had to split up because of European regulations. Several competitors make use of this same logistic infrastructure which serves a common purpose. Although the government department had their own negotiation process, we still shared many rules and regulations. However both organizations have their own wage structure and the government level is not the same as ours. This creates tension, on a day-to-day basis, between the people working in the government and people in our company who sometimes work closely together. Two other union leaders, Stef and Egon, had done their homework well, presenting an analysis of the present and an extensive description of the future they wanted. During the process they tried to hang on to their ideas and come back to their plan but now nobody accepted their invitation. Their disadvantage was that the group they represented was one of the smallest.

The issue of job security and job flexibility

On the April 13, 2004 we had an EXB strategy meeting. The subjects I presented did not arouse much discussion. However, it was clear that some of the members strongly opposed Job Security and Flexibility (JSF). Although JSF had been agreed for the more than 7,000 staff members of the General Services Division in the last labor agreement, my impression was that some of the EXB had agreed to this against their will or were overruled. This time they wanted to make sure that this would not happen again. However, I was convinced of the importance of extending JSF to other parts of the company because of the new distribution system we would be installing in the coming years. I felt that extending JSF in this way would reduce the possibility of union members organizing strikes, even if their unions had reached an agreement, as had happened in 2001.

We were not alone in this line of thinking. Wilthagen (1998) introduced the term "flexicurity" as a new paradigm for labor market policy reform. He describes this concept as a tradeoff between labor market flexibility and increased national social security models. He states that flexicurity could be considered as an implementation strategy for transitional labor markets under government supervision. The main purpose at that stage was to create social systems more open for transitory states between gainful employment and productive non-market activities to alleviate structural unemployment. Later Wilthagen (2002) extended this thinking not only to transitions between work and social security situations but to the emerging of the flexibility-security nexus in and between companies. In our company this line of thinking was transferred into the JSF proposition.

The first ideas of exchanging Job Security for Flexibility and mobility came up in 2003. The General Services Division, which had been through the major trauma of 2000, had to reach a new labor agreement and there was a real necessity to discuss changes in working patterns. Every discussion about this subject ended in a stalemate, because people were afraid of losing their jobs when organizational change and reduction of staff were discussed. By analyzing pension schemes and dates of retirement the management of this division, in those days responsible for their own agreement, had figured out that natural reduction of staff numbers matched the business plan forecast of the next eight years and they decided to offer this security. Combined with a reasonable wage increase, stability on the worker front was restored and management could start working on the next phase of plans.

The purpose of the negotiation I was leading was to combine all labor agreements in order to create a new "one group feeling". Differences in legal position, with some people having JSF and others not, would hinder us in the discussions about job integration, more output with less personnel, and new working schemes. Every time the subject arose in board meetings, feelings of animosity occurred. By creating a hostile atmosphere the willingness of others to talk about the matter was reduced.

In our negotiation team we had made calculations of what would happen if we honored the request of the unions to extend the JSF offer to the staff of other Specialized Divisions, which would enable us to start talks about the integration of jobs between the General Services and other Specialized Divisions. It turned out that it would easily fit the business plan forecast so we decided to support the idea and to present it in the next EXB meeting. During this EXB meeting, the discussion about JSF followed two directions. First, for some, there was a feeling that extension of the working sphere of JSF could bring the necessary flexibility (with a stronger agreement and better contract), given that organizational change was inevitable. Second, other members reported that the experiences with flexibility so far had been disappointing. There was another complication. If JSF was extended to all the company's national divisions, the international division would also press for it. I was requested to present an inventory of all types of JSF agreements for one of the next EXB meetings. There was also misunderstanding on the current agreement and not enough knowledge about the staff reduction due to normal retirement. We promised to provide the necessary information for regional, national and international operations.

Although we later provided detailed information, the members of the EXB still did not give us the impression that they agreed with us on JSF. We, the negotiation team, tried again to give improved and clearer information. I tried to explain that many of the other subjects were directed by new government rules and regulations and that our main goal was to create as much room as possible for future change in the organization and possible lower costs. Eventually, the EXB agreed on JSF for those groups of employees working in the same field. JSF, previously agreed upon for the operational staff of the General Services Division, was to be extended to service groups of other Specialized Divisions. The negotiation team would prepare a memorandum on how staff of the General Services Division were distributed over the regions in the country and what it would mean to add the other service people. Decision making processes moved slowly forward but there was still a feeling of "it is 'yes', but...?" The atmosphere during the discussion of this issue continued to be tense and reflect the pattern of power relations.

Because of the concerns of Boris, I organized a meeting with one of the directors of the government logistic department to discuss JSF. Also, they would be greatly affected by the outcome of our agreement and we needed to investigate where serving our interests would become counterproductive for them. In the meantime, the negotiation team had developed a strong coherence; we even had some harsh discussions and real conflicts, but came out stronger. I want to stress the fact that what we normally take for granted, everyday conversation, played an important role in all phases of the process.

As the patterning within and between the different groupings evolved, it became clearer and clearer that the JSF issue was leading to a more and more polarized conflict situation between several of the participants. The atmosphere at meetings was grim and the discussion itself was leading nowhere. During one of the EXB meetings, I asked if there were other reasons for the opposition that had not yet been disclosed. This question led to a hostile atmosphere and did not take us any further. We were stuck. However, my team and I were convinced that an understanding on JSF would help the company to move forward in the coming years and also help us finalize the negotiations. In October 2004 one of the unions sent us a letter demanding job security for all staff. This was the first time the unions had brought the subject up for discussion.

So, what I want to draw attention to here, as we slowly approached negotiations with the unions, is the tension, with its potential for polarized conflict, within the EXB and also with closely related companies.

Conflict: individuals and groups

Reflecting now on these events, I can see how we in the negotiating team identified the three most important groups involved in these negotiations as our own team, the EXB and the union leaders. There were many other groups also involved but they did not have the same influence. Individuals participated in a number of different groups. Many of the discussions in these groupings took the form of explorative conflict as we worked through our differences and although the potential for polarized conflict was never far away in any of these groupings, the only serious potential for polarized conflict emerged in the EXB, where the discussion stagnated and explorative conflict was neglected and avoided. So what do other authors in the sociology and organizational literatures have to say about the role of groups in emerging conflict or the prevention thereof?

Coser (1956) explains the effects of conflict on groups in two ways. First, conflict sets boundaries between groups within a social system, creating awareness of separateness and thus creating the identity of groups within the system. Second, conflict reinforces group cohesion. He argues that conflict establishes the distinction between the "in-group" and the "out-groups" so giving rise to the development of the identity of persons. Coser makes a distinction between realistic and unrealistic conflicts. Realistic conflicts are means toward a specific result whereas non-realistic conflicts, although still evolving in interaction, are not caused by the antagonists but by the need for tension release of at least one of them. Non-realistic elements in realistic conflict situations increase the intensity of the conflict.

Rapoport (1974) starts with an extensive analysis of conflict in nature in general, as the struggle for existence, evolution and survival. When dealing with conflict he says you first have to identify the conflicting parties. In doing so it seems most natural to identify individuals as the basic conflicting parties because if all members of a group have the same aspirations there will be no problem. When some members of the group want to achieve goals and purposes for their own benefit, problems will arise.

Rapoport focuses on systemic theories of conflict, where it is not the individual psyche which is at the center of attention but group processes not subject to control by single individuals. When looking at the role of individuals, Rapoport draws, among others, on Thomas Hobbes' picture of human life as the war of everyone against everyone. In Hobbes' model, individuals are not differentiated from each other, in which case the focus of attention is not on individual psychology but on systemic effect. For example, Rapoport considers the "psychologies" of actors larger than individuals, in particular highly organized social "organisms" like states. The soldier sent out to a war obeys the command even if he does not want to. Coser focuses more on the individual human being, whereas Rapoport chooses a systemic and group approach, pointing to Hegel's idea that contradiction is unavoidable in the process of logical progression toward the truth and that this contradiction is in its essence also a concept for conflict.

Mastenbroek (1994) describes his methods for intervention in terms of four stereotypical patterns of relationship connected to certain behavior, problems and frictions. Based on this assumption Mastenbroek (1994: 206–8) distinguishes four types of conflict solving behavior shown in Table 3.1.

Glasl (1999) generally sees two opposite positions in dealing with conflict: conflict avoidance and battle. The first attitude suppresses all forms of conflict and will result in a negative influence on the working atmosphere. In the second

Table 3.1 Types of conflict solving behavior

Types of conflict	*Effective behavior*
Instrumental conflicts, which are business- or target oriented	Problem analysis, efficient meeting and decision-making processes
Social emotional conflicts, which focus on identity	Empathy and open communication
Negotiation conflicts, concerned with the distribution of scarce goods	Negotiate
Power and dependency conflicts, focused on securing position or improving positions in relation to others	Structuring mutual dependency

Source: Mastenbroek (1994).

attitude conflicts will go on until social coherence in the group is lost completely. Glasl focuses more on the individual in the group and less on conflict between groups. His most important question is whether the person has a conflict or whether the conflict has the person. In other words, does the person still have control over himself? When the conflict has control over the person, this person will be guided as if by an invisible hand and will transform the image of the other. In a conflict situation there is self-infection.

He provides many intervention techniques based on nine different levels of escalation to handle these kinds of situations with the strong belief that awareness about conflict can prevent it from emerging or can solve it.

1   Hardening: Concentrate on issues, suitable communication methods relieve the strain, loosening to allow to return to the positive qualities of people involved.
2   Debate and polemics: Disabling the polarized powers, from fighting for dominance to debate, from compulsive ping-pong to self directed action.
3   Actions not words: Strengthening empathy, loosening the crystallized roles, clarifying discrepancies between verbal and non-verbal messages.
4   Images and coalitions: Correcting distorted perceptions which disable perceptive mechanisms, dissolving fateful role attributions.

After this point professional help is advised.

5   Loss of face: Process consultation or process counseling.
6   Strategies of threat: loosen or break interlocking of the conflicting parties.
7   Limited destructive blows: Mediation in the classic sense is required.
8   Fragmentation of the enemy: Voluntary arbitration.
9   Together into the abyss: Mobilization of superior power.

(Glasl, 1999: 123)

Glasl works out the interventions in great detail which can be helpful in recognizing the occurring situation, but we will have to bear in mind that every situation will be slightly different from any other and requires a different approach, a basic assumption when working in terms of complex responsive processes.

Elias (1978) describes interaction between human groupings in terms of patterns of power relations in which people are included and excluded from particular groupings. It is this process of power relating which creates the identity of the individual ("I" identity) and the group ("we" identity). One's sense of personal identity is closely connected with the "we" and "they" relationship within and between groups. In this way the identity creation of the "I" and the "we" are closely connected. Griffin (2002: 195) describes the "I" and the "we" as emerging identity in the tension of the direct experience of relationships between human beings in the unity of the social act and relates this to complex responsive processes. He shows that conflict is a natural process in the recognizing of one's own identity in the other and the other in oneself and that recreating one's identity cannot be realized without the struggle of entering into conflict. Griffin focuses strongly on the relation of conflict and identity. The transformation of identity through conflict is an intense process because conflict holds a high level of emotion and tension. Griffin develops his line of thinking from the leadership perspective. I think there is no leadership without emotion, and emotion like conflict transforms identity. Coping with this phenomenon is one of the major aspects of leadership. Taking the views of Griffin into account opens up new possibilities in processes of negotiations. I will now review some of the experimental processes, which helped us to develop negotiations in an explorative way.

Preparations for the negotiations continue

I had my first meeting with Charles, the leader of one of the unions, in December 2004. This meeting had been postponed six times during the previous ten months. To my great surprise, and probably also to his, we got along very well, which immediately led to a few other meetings. In previous labor agreement negotiations this union had been the hardest to deal with. After my meetings with Charles we organized an informal dinner meeting with all the union leaders to get to know each other better and to exchange general knowledge. It was a successful first step that involved the exchange of much personal information. We took our time to build up a relationship and to create something of a common feeling. At the end of the dinner we planned the first official meeting to exchange company information.

There were also other ways in which we engaged the unions. For example we organized theme groups and later we organized a conference.

Theme groups

Early in 2005, after our second explorative dinner meeting with the union leaders, our negotiation team reviewed the interaction between the unions, noticing the competition and sometimes the tense atmosphere when they started negotiating between themselves. Those are the moments that one feels that polarized conflict is still lying around the corner. In the light of this, we proposed setting up small combined theme groups involving the different unions and ourselves, to investigate in detail four main topics:

1   Job security combined with job reduction and job flexibility
2   Pensions
3   One labor agreement
4   Conditions related to sickness and the disabled

All unions agreed to participate in these groups and to investigate the boundaries between the major subject areas. The outcome of this meeting guaranteed us the desired delay of the beginning of the real negotiations. We had the impression that time would help us in building up not only personal relations but also working relations with union members and leaders.

Our intention in setting up the smaller theme groups was to provide forums where we could discuss the major issues together with union representatives and explore the situations we all found ourselves in. The last thing I wanted to happen was that we forced ourselves into real negotiations. The government was so unclear about future regulations on our main negotiation points that, given a huge demonstration of hundreds of thousands of union members against government policy, especially on pension regulations, starting negotiations too soon could easily bring us into a polarized conflict situation. Avoiding the formulation of a strategy right at the start is not a common procedure during negotiations. In normal negotiation processes people tend to take up starting positions on what they would like to realize as a best outcome and the party which can hold on to this starting position the longest makes the most out of the negotiation (Karrass, 1974). In not taking this position, the process went in a different direction where parties were investigating together what new government regulations would mean for everybody and what an objective point of view might be. Because of the universal uncertainty, the risk of going into polarized conflict about unclear negotiation points was so high that we intuitively chose another approach.

Another example of how we slowly prepared for the negotiations is the conference we organized.

The conference

During a short conference on complex responsive processes at the Complexity and Management Centre of the University of Hertfordshire near London, I was given a suggestion by one of the participants to contact a consultant on union participation in organizational change. At the same time, Boris proposed having a conference to develop a recovery plan for the complete sector. The members of the negotiating team favored the idea to create joint experiments with the unions.

As a result I made an appointment with the consultant together with two people of the negotiating team and we met him in London. He talked to us about the privatization process of the British energy and electricity industry where he was involved in the change program of one of the sectors. These public sector organizations had to be transformed into a commercial company. From the start of the process, management tried to involve the unions in playing an active part. This was not easy to say the least, because unions were afraid of losing control, influence and power and were organized in a bureaucratic way. They organized brainstorm sessions with employees of this "future" company about many subjects and invited union leaders to take part in these meetings. During the meetings all hierarchical levels were mixed. Special attention was paid to involve so called opinion leaders or "trouble-makers", often also active members of the unions. As a result of these meetings ten conferences in the country were organized inviting all other employees, to increase the general level of participation. People were able to convince each other that there were no hidden agendas, and the results of these conferences contributed strongly to a smoother change process than expected. Looking at our case, the expert suggested inviting the unions into the strategic thinking process of the company based on his positive experiences during a massive change program. Also a conference with union leaders and opinion leaders about the future of the company, which was similar to Boris' earlier idea for a joint conference, supported the process.

The members of the EXB were enthusiastic about a conference to discuss the future of the Group with union leaders and opinion formers. The negotiation team suggested that the CEO should take the lead at the conference to signal a separation between the conference and the actual negotiations. It was clear that the negotiations and the conference would influence each other and that the conference would give us an additional opportunity to work with the union representatives. Soon after, we had a meeting with the union leaders to prepare for the conference. Although there was always some tension at these meetings, the union leaders were very enthusiastic about the idea of a conference. Ellis, a colleague of Godfried, then joined the organizing team. She had been employed by one of the unions and had a good sense of what was going on there. One of our ideas was to create preparation teams consisting of union leaders, union members and ourselves. I suggested that it would be wise to involve the HRM managers of the divisions because they still felt excluded. This suggestion was accepted. We formulated a communication plan and I undertook to inform EXB members about the conference plan.

When we organized this conference for the beginning of February 2005, the unions agreed to postpone the negotiations, even though the old agreement had expired by then. This was exactly what we wanted and indeed it served a mutual purpose for both the unions and ourselves. We hoped that the conference would improve our working relations with the unions. Boris suggested a conference preparation meeting with the participants sharing dreams about the company's future.

The conference itself was organized as an open space gathering (Owen, 1997), a meeting instrument we often use and was attended by more than 150 participants, including management, union leaders and union members. We gathered all information around dreams of participants in advance, created a marketplace where people could express their interest in discussing certain topics and in the end had a public forum where people could express their ideas or concerns based on the discussions. In between we held a "press conference" with interviews with union leaders and our CEO. During the conference it was possible for everybody, working anywhere in the country, to communicate through an internet connection. This even went on for extra days after the conference. In the end we informed all employees through our journal and a special bulletin about the results. A second conference was to be organized before the end of the year.

This turned out to be a useful exercise because it led to an open exchange of information; although some people did have doubts about the use of sharing dreams to initiate discussions because of the risk of speculating about an idealized future shorn of any obstacles to achieving it. However, the discussions we had did reduce fears of threats and manipulation, because everybody could take part. After sharing many dreams, the discussion moved quickly to the day-to-day working situation of drivers, mechanics, conductors and customer service people which formed a common context for all of us. Without the dream sessions, this might not have happened so easily.

There was an unexpected interruption in the development of relationships with the unions after the conference. Boris, one of the union leaders, provided members of Parliament with incomplete information about a calculation model from the conference. This led to a severe confrontation between Boris and the company after which we had a serious discussion with him. Godfried explained to the negotiation team that passing on information by the unions to outsiders was always a risk and had often happened in previous years. The team formed the view that this action would have to be responded to and so proposed a very interesting early retirement scheme, making it clear that this was not a shared success of both the unions and the company. Boris understood the message from the negotiation team and promised that information leaks would not happen again. We knew that we were moving at the edge of possible polarized conflict and had to inform the other unions of what happened.

Negotiations, agreement and some surprises

Although I was the leader of the negotiating team, it turned out during the first round of the negotiations that Godfried took the initiative of chairing the meeting. This was not prearranged but, rather, happened in a very natural way and he continued to take this role at all other meetings, after members of the negotiation team decided that they all felt comfortable with it. Due to his expert knowledge on many subjects he was already doing much of the talking, which he did with much talent. This development gave me the chance to play a bigger role in discussing ideas and content. Godfried and I had our final meeting with the CEO about our mandate on March 23, 2005. JSF was still the most important issue. We wrote a final memorandum highlighting all the items we were to discuss with the unions and suggested another discussion with the EXB because the JSF subject was still so sensitive. However, everybody felt that the information was clear and that we had talked about it enough.

During the third round of negotiations on March 24, 2005 we were slowly moving forward on all subjects. We exchanged much technical information and in the end the questions on JSF and the required organizational change regarding EDS brought some life to the meeting. The discussion offered us the possibility of clarifying our ideas and reducing the unions' fear that people would feel threatened by the reductions in staff and changes in work patterns required by EDS. We explained that we could reduce our workforce by 1,700 operational members in a completely natural way between 2005 and January 1, 2011. That is why we could offer job security to operational staff of other divisions.

However, we made it clear that the same amount of work had to be done with 1,700 fewer employees due to the investment we would be making in the new distribution systems. All understood that this had to be our main mission for the coming years.

One of the unions wanted to extend job security to the operational team of the International Division. The managing director of this division had given job security under certain conditions to his staff and agreed that we could bring the subject into our negotiations. I explained the situation in a telephone call to our CEO to get his approval for this arrangement. Afterward I discovered that he had misunderstood how many board members were directly involved in this discussion, which led to a conflict after finalizing the agreement.

On April 20, 2005, the last round of the negotiations started at 10 am. A problem arose due to a mistake or misunderstanding by us at 1.30 am in the morning of the next day and there was an intense and very long silence, at least it felt that way. The leader of one of the unions gave in immediately and solved the problem in the blink of an eye. This was one of the most remarkable moments during the whole negotiation period and showed the atmosphere we had been able to create. At 2.30 am that day we had an agreement and by 4 am Godfried and I could sign the papers together with the Union Leaders. After having a beer together we prepared news releases for the newspapers, radio and television. No conflict, no extra tension.

All news stations talked about a revolutionary agreement supported by unions and the company. Remarkable was the quiet, almost silent way the whole process had moved forward. Compared to many times in the past when we hit the newspapers with controversial news and conflict, this was a big surprise for many people. Some did not even know we had already started the negotiations, although unions presented results on their Internet sites on a day-to-day basis. All union members supported the outcome and on June 3, 2005 we presented the follow up of the negotiations to the EXB.

However there was also an unexpected development. Some members of the EXB still had doubts about the outcome, mainly because extension of job security was part of the agreement. (The decision was made on 23rd of March 2005 and communicated by internal memo to all EXB members, but it remained controversial.) It was strange to experience a certain distance, which surfaced during some of the regular meetings. My feeling of success was diminished and I wondered if and how I should communicate this to my team. In fact I had a bad weekend, especially because all newspapers in the country were complimenting us on the results. I was able to express my astonishment at the attitude of some in an EXB meeting a few days later. We discussed in more detail the EXB processes accompanying the negotiations and why some of the EXB members felt ignored. When it came to the issue of JSF, it was clear that whatever the outcome, some members would be against it. The CEO had interpreted the extended mandate for the operational staff of the International Division during our telephone conversation in another way, but their managing director did not leave any doubt that he agreed with our approach. The outcome of the meeting was that the JSF subject was so sensitive that another EXB meeting after March 23 would have been wiser.

Sometime later, there was another surprise. The negotiations of the logistics department of the government were not our direct responsibility. Their management, however, was not able to reach an agreement on terms and wages and on June 17, 2005 this department went on strike. Although we were not directly involved in this part of the negotiation process, we could have been more aware of the pending risks and perhaps we could have tried to have more influence on their process directly or via our negotiation partners. Luckily they soon reached an agreement.

Local interaction and global patterns

This chapter has described organizational negotiation processes comprising more than 100 meetings and discussions. I have left out many, many details, but I hope I have included enough to show that such processes are messy and full of unexpected sidesteps. How it all evolves depends on the specific contexts the parties find themselves in and on many coincidences. A key question for me is this: what made it possible to work at the edge of polarized conflict without such conflict actually arising during the negotiations? I think the answer has to do with building up good relations, which took much time and energy. In the end it was this that helped us to avoid polarized conflict and achieve a result that benefited both the company and its employees.

Instead of following standard negotiation procedures we created opportunities for discussion amounting to opening the door to explorative conflict; it is this engagement in explorative conflict rather than suppressing or avoiding conflict, which creates the greater possibilities of avoiding polarized conflict. There is risk taking involved, because explorative conflict approaches the edges of polarized conflict, but in doing so we reduced the risk of an outbreak. Although this is a specific example to do with union negotiations, I suggest that it has general implications for many other management processes where complicated negotiations inevitably raise the prospect of conflict. I would say that during the period of the negotiations, my colleagues and I operated quite intuitively and in the process created a different approach to negotiating. As the leader, I think I tried to stimulate working at the edge of polarized conflict where creativity evolved in local interaction (self organization) from which there emerged the global, population-wide patterns (strategy) of better understanding with the unions and a successful agreement, as well as global patterns of a divided EXB and a strike at the logistic government department. Let me explain.

As I have said before, several groups played important roles in the overall processes of the negotiation. The EXB was responsible for the Group as a whole, that is, the head office and all the divisions. The negotiating team had to relate to the EXB and it also had working relations with divisions and HRM departments. The Union leaders acted as one group but also as separate entities for the people they represented and we in the negotiation team had to develop relationships with them individually and collectively. Many other groups played a role during these negotiations and then there were policy makers and politicians in the central government who were making decisions of direct relevance to our negotiations. Again we had some interaction with all of these groupings. In terms of activity, all of these groupings consisted of relatively small numbers of people, sometimes with the same people in more than one grouping, who accomplished whatever it was that they accomplished in ongoing conversations, in relationships, with each other. All of this can be described as local interactions (Stacey, 2005), or more technically, as self-organization. The narrative in this paper has pointed to some of these local interactions.

Those working in the natural complexity sciences have been particularly concerned with the relationship between self-organizing, that is, local, interactions (micro activities) and global or widespread patterns (the macro). For example, Prigogine (1996: 60) became convinced that macroscopic irreversibility of time was the manifestation of the randomness of probabilistic processes on a microscopic scale. Also, in an interview with Van Maris (2005) on computer simulations of the self-organizing development of vowel systems, Bart de Boer argued that global structures emerge only through interactions on the local level, without any outside influence and without a prearranged hierarchical structure. When I (the local), drop something in a pond (the global), water starts moving away in circles and in moving it will encounter obstacles (other locals), such as a patch of leaves, a rock, or even a few ducks, on the other side of the pond. Patterns will emerge across the pond.

Elias (1978), writing long before the complexity sciences appeared, took a similar view of human interaction. He explains that (1) development of technology; (2) social organization, the twin processes of increasing differentiation and increasing integration; and (3) the civilizing process cannot be understood in terms of parallel increase in what he calls three types of control leading to a predictable future. Especially in the civilizing process changes in self control take place which can be nonlinear. Elias says that looking at the past makes it possible to see how present forms of society have emerged from earlier forms but that this has no pre-existing aim or significance. Trends do not take a straight course and very often develop via severe conflicts. It is beyond human power or foresight to carry out changes in social structures. Elias refers in a way to types of local interaction leading to an unpredictable form of tomorrow's (global) society.

I argue that it makes sense of my experience of the negotiations to think in this way about the many local interactions, the many meetings and events, through which widespread, global patterns emerged. In other words, strategies, as global patterns emerged in the continuous thinking and discussion involving all of us in many local situations during the negotiation process through which we were reconstructing every step we took. However, in all our local interactions, we were also keeping in mind "the big picture". We were very aware of a number of global patterns: our Group's contracts with central and regional governments; the financial resources and results; our clients and their representative organizations; our own organizational structure; and so on. So in our many local interactions we were co-constructing the emergent global patterns but at the same time we were taking into our local interactions our generalized interpretations of these global patterns. These generalizations then were constraining us. These generalized global patterns, both internal to our company and external to it, were most of the time beyond our control.

When we take a complex responsive process view we focus on communication between humans. This immediately leads to diversity and unpredictability. This makes us look at organizations as ongoing temporal processes of human communicative interaction.

> Social forces, social structures, routines and habits can all be understood as generalizations that are particularized over and over again in each specific situation we are in.... Furthermore these generalizations are often idealized and come to form the cult values we repeatedly have to functionalize in our interactions. This way of understanding routines and habits focuses attention on the inevitably conflictual nature of particularizing the general and the idealized.
>
> (Stacey, 2005: 19)

It is the idealization of our imaginatively created unity which makes us experience values; the voluntary compulsions that serve as criteria for good and bad actions (Dewey, 1934). Mead (1934) talked about the functionalization of idealized cult values to give the values we make use of in our day-to-day life and this always gives rise to conflict, which will show itself in interaction. This is true for the kind of negotiation processes I have been describing, as well as for the implications on strategic developments of the company as a whole.

At the EXB meetings some of the members tried to hold on to the cult value, "companies do not give away job security". However, the reality was that more than 7,000 employees had already been given job security. It was the proposed functionalization of this cult value involving the addition of a further 1,500 employees to the scheme that evoked the different opinions. Some tried to limit diversity by holding on to the cult value in an absolute sense, while others were trying to functionalize it. These differences of opinion led to attempts by some to engage in explorative conflict as part of a normal discussion, while others were moving toward polarized conflict. Power plays an important role in who will take up which position. The approach of Griffin (2002) and Mead (1934) is one in which people engage in explorative conflict which often comes close to working at the edge of polarized conflict. When, in a discussion, people try to hold on to cult values at all costs the explorative conflict phase will not take place and people will immediately enter polarized conflict and get stuck.

Negotiations always took place in local interactions from which there emerged global patterns that were in turn taken up in local interactions, eventually leading to a final agreement between the parties. The conference idea and the joint theme groups enriched the local interactions so that global patterns emerged that were different to what they otherwise probably would have been. Leaders initiate intentions in the present and develop initiatives for the future, but what emerges is also created in the responses of others who participated in the preparation, the conference and the work in the theme groups. Initiating these patterning processes became the trademark of this negotiation period, where the emergence of conflict was far more present in our internal individual interactions.

Conclusion

What is this narrative about? It is a story of how a team worked together in negotiations about the terms and conditions of a labor agreement for our company's employees. These negotiations were different from previous ones because the lead from the company side of the negotiations was taken by an operational managing director, instead of a professional negotiator from the Human Resources department and because one agreement had to be negotiated for the whole company, replacing separate agreements for different parts of the company.

Two important contextual matters formed the background for the negotiations. The memory of the 1999 agreement to which the unions agreed but which was then undermined by the emergence of dissenting sub groupings of union members leading to a damaging strike. The new negotiation team was strongly motivated to prevent a repetition of this. Also there is the strategy we are developing of installing electronic distribution systems. It was important that whatever we agreed with the unions should not impede, but rather assist, the implementation of strategic changes affecting the jobs and work patterns of very large numbers of employees.

The story is about negotiations with the unions, but it is not only a story of labor relations, but also a story of how conflict is implicated in all decision making processes, which shows the centrality of conflict in management processes. I have tried to make clear how general points on the development of conflict are of relevance to management and leadership generally in all situations and the roles of individuals and groups in conflict situations. In the literature I turned to, I distinguished three types of conflict:

- Polarized conflict
- Preventive or Repressive conflict
- Natural or Normative conflict

The negotiation team avoided starting with clear negotiating positions because the potential for polarized conflict is very high when people do this in conditions of great uncertainty. Preventive or repressive conflict almost always ends up directly in polarized conflict, so simply negating the differences was not the solution. Instead we created as many opportunities as we could in developing relationships and discussing and engaging differences, in doing so we created another form of conflict as a normal process in creating identity:

- Explorative conflict

We were trying to engage in explorative conflict. As the leader of the team I stimulated moving forward in search of this type of conflict and initiated organizational circumstances in working with subgroups and a conference in which opinions and differences could be explored. This approach differs from the ones described by the authors in the literature I turned to, where prevention of conflict is seen as a manageable process, but conflict itself is seen as an autonomous phenomenon in the process of interacting. Exploring difference can quickly and easily erupt into polarized conflict. Explorative conflict is in a sense always at the edge of polarized conflict, which is why many people avoid it, because when they object to discussing sensitive differences it can "open up a can of worms". Taking risks is inherent in engaging with explorative conflict in order to reduce the potential for polarized conflict.

I also tried to make a link between conflict and Mead's generalization/particularization and idealization (cult value)/functionalization theory. When people, in their relating to or negotiating with each other, directly apply generalizations or cult values, then there is no possibility other than polarized conflict. As soon as we start taking account of the specific time and situation we are in, we are particularizing or functionalizing the general and the ideal. This requires continuing conversation in which we engage in explorative conflict. We still have our different positions but now we are negating the simple negation, the polarization, and exploring how we can obtain something of what we want that makes sense for both of us in the specific situation we find ourselves in. The opposition, the conflict, is then potentially transformed into a novel arrangement we can all live with.

Union and employer representatives always start negotiations with ideal propositions from their own standpoint, strongly influenced by cult values cherished by each party. During our negotiations intensive focus on improving relations between the involved parties led to a high degree of particularizing and functionalizing of the general and the ideal departing points on both sides. In this case through explorative conflict it produced a successful outcome, although there is nothing inevitable about this. In the end other interdependent factors came into play in the emergence of polarized conflict in the Executive Board and the repressed conflict of the logistic government department, the last leading to a one day strike after all. These last events point to the complexity of organizational life and show there are no simple recipes for "getting it right".

References

Coser, L. A. (1956) *The Functions of Social Conflict*, New York: The Free Press.
Dewey, J. (1934) *A Common Faith*, New Haven, CT: Yale University Press.

Elias, N. (1978) *What is Sociology?*, London: Hutchinson & Co.

Glasl, F. (1999) *A First-Aid Kit for Handling Conflict*, New York: Hawthorn Press.

Griffin, D. (2002) *The Emergence of Leadership: Linking Self-Organization and Ethics*, London: Routledge.

Iterson, Van A., Mastenbroek, W., Newton, T. and Smith, D. (eds.) (2002) *The Civilized Organization: Norbert Elias and the Future of Organization Studies*, Amsterdam and Philadelphia: John Benjamin Publishing Company.

Karrass, C. L. (1974) *Give and Take: The Complete Guide to Negotiating Strategies and Tactics*, New York: Ty Crowell Co.

Maris, B. Van (2005) "Aparte Klanken, simulatie van klinkerontwikkeling wijst op zelforganisatie taal", *NRC Handelsblad*, Rotterdam: PCM Uitgevers, zaterdag 7 mei 2005: 43.

Mastenbroek, W. F. G. (1994) *Conflict Management and Organization Development*, Chichester: John Wiley & Son Ltd.

Mead, G. H. (1934) *Mind, Self, & Society*, London: The University of Chicago Press.

Owen, H. (1997) *Open Space Technology: A User's Guide*, San Francisco: Berrett-Koehler Publishers, Inc.

Prigogine, I. (1997) *The End of Certainty: Time, Chaos, and the New Laws of Nature*, New York: The Free Press.

Rapoport, A. (1974) *Conflict in Man-made Environments*, Harmondsworth: Penguin Books Ltd.

Schermerhorn, R., Hunt, J. G. and Osborn, R. N. (1991) *Managing Organizational Behavior*, New York: John Wiley & Sons Inc.

Shaw, P. (2002) *Changing Conversations in Organizations: A complexity approach to change*, London: Routledge.

Stacey, R. D. (2003) *Strategic Management and Organisational Dynamics* (4th ed), Harlow, England: Pearson Education Limited.

Stacey, R. D. (ed.) (2005) *Experiencing Emergence in Organizations: Local Interaction and the Emergence of Global Pattern*, London: Routledge.

Walton, R. E. (1972) "Interorganizational decision making and identity conflict", in M. Tuite, R. Chisholm and M. Radnor (eds.) *International Decision Making*, Chicago: Aldine Publishing Company.

Walton, R. E., Dutton, J. M. and Cafferty, T. P. (1969) "Organizational context and inter-departmental conflict", *Administrative Science Quarterly* 8: 73–84.

Wilthagen, T. (1988) "Social integration by transitional labor markets", in *Flexicurity: A New Paradigm for Labor Market Policy Reform?*, Berlin: Wissenschaftszentrum für Sozialforschung.

Wilthagen, T. (2002) *The Flexibility-Security Nexus: New Approaches to Regulating Employment and Labor Markets*, Tilburg: OSA/Institute for Labor Studies, Tilburg University.

Editors' introduction to Chapter 4

Iver Drabæk, an independent consultant, describes the ethical issue arising in relation to an invitation to work as an auditor required to verify information provided by companies for a database of ethical companies. This information formed the basis of their Corporate Social Responsibility (CSR) Database. Drabæk draws attention to the potential conflict between his need to earn an income, on the one hand, and his misgivings about the principle of the Database itself and the adequacy of the budget made available to pay for the verification. His misgivings about the Database arise from his view that too many compromises had been made in the interest of making registration on the database attractive to companies. In his view, these compromises greatly diminished the usefulness of the Database in guiding the decisions of customers. However, he did approve of the idea in principle and he did need the income from the project. He too, therefore, was faced with compromises and decided to carry out the work. Drabæk takes the situation he faced and the struggle he had to make an ethical decision as a reflection of much wider patterns in the auditing and accountancy professions. He draws attention to the cult values of these professions which center on independence and objectivity. However, advancement within these professions depends upon the ability to generate income and auditing and accountancy relationships afford the opportunity to generate consultancy income. The values of independence/objectivity therefore come into conflict with the need to generate income, so creating situations in which some form of compromise becomes a practical necessity. Drabæk's main concern in this chapter is that of how we are to think about the matter of compromise in professional and organizational life.

Normally, to compromise is understood to mean to settle for less than the ideal and therefore often involves acting in a manner that conflicts with one's values. There is then something inevitable about compromise when it comes to practical action in the world. Drabæk argues that the activity of reflecting upon the different aspects and consequences of compromises leads one to impose constraints on what one does so that the compromise becomes acceptable. In this way the process of compromising enables action to be taken. Drabæk, therefore, argues that compromising is the process of constraining and enabling actions and so involves power relations. Compromising is the process of negotiating the constraints people encounter in their ordinary, everyday interactions and it is this that enables people to move on together rather than remain stuck. This is in contrast to the normal elevation of "no compromise" as a sign of strength. Far from being a sign of strength, the "no compromise" stance is guaranteed to keep people stuck in repetitive patterns, while the "compromise" stance enables them to move forward together in constrained ways. Drabæk draws on Mead to argue further that compromising can involve sacrificing the narrow self in the development of a larger self which makes it possible for new patterns of interaction to emerge. The simplistic equation of compromise with unethical action is thus untenable.

4 Compromising as processes of moving forward in organizations

Iver Drabæk

I work as an independent consultant and, at the time of this story, my project workload was satisfactory; but future prospects were not as good as I could have hoped, because some projects had been postponed and others had not materialized. Against this background, I met with Judy, a manager at a Danish consumer information organization, DCIC, who was in charge of maintaining a database of ethical companies subscribing to the Corporate Social Responsibility (CSR) Database. The purpose of the meeting was to discuss a potential consulting opportunity, which was a project involving the verification of information supplied by companies to be listed on the CSR Database, justifying their inclusion on the database of "ethical" companies. I had mixed feelings about this project. The CSR Database had been partially developed by a former close colleague from the days of my working for a large international consulting organization, and I had been involved in discussions of the proposal submitted by our organization to DCIC. However, I had not taken part in the actual project execution, and so felt that I was sufficiently independent of the CSR Database to accept a job as third-party verifier. Furthermore, I had always had serious doubts about the CSR Database concept, which I shall explore here before going on to describe my meeting with Judy.

The Corporate Social Responsibility Database concept

The CSR Database was developed by DCIC, which now operates it. It was designed to be a tool enabling ethically aware consumers to make informed decisions about their purchases from socially responsible companies, as well as providing a platform for companies and other organizations to communicate publicly about their initiatives on social responsibility and corporate governance. Companies and organizations sign up as members by application, and their application is initially granted by DCIC. Subsequently, however, the members are subjected to external control by spot verifications to check on how far they are in the process of implementing the CSR Database and what specific steps they are taking to incorporate social responsibility into their business operations. The CSR Database is based on the international conventions of the International Labor Organization, a specialized agency of the UN, and on rules and regulations on employee rights and health and safety at work. The results of the verification check on each member are made available to the public on the Internet.

I strongly support the intention behind the CSR Database but, in my opinion, DCIC made far too many compromises in the initial stages of the project; and this severely inhibits its potential success. The project targets consumers and therefore the information about a range of relevant consumer goods needs to be easily accessible, understandable, relevant and up to date. Consequently a broad participation of companies is needed. There are, however, two inherent problems in this. First, consumers buy products, not companies; so if information is classified by company rather than product, consumers may well not get the relevant information on their first search of the database. Second, companies are hesitant to pay large membership fees or to use significant internal resources in providing and updating the information, particularly if they are not sure that it will be used by consumers.

As is the case with many other projects, the resources available for project development in the end determined certain priorities. Priority number one was to recruit member companies, which meant that the membership had to be relatively cheap and that procedures for providing information to the database had to be simple. In my opinion, this made the information available for the consumers inadequate and irrelevant – a potential catastrophe for a consumer information project! The DCIC believed that if the project attracted sufficient members, then the content could be improved later from new member fees. Although skeptical of the current design and organizational back-up for the Database, and concerned that it was more or less useless for consumers, I did believe that the process of providing the information itself could have some value for the participating companies in helping them to understand what CSR meant for them.

The role of the auditor

Fundamental to the credibility of the CSR Database is the validity of the data. Although data submission is based on self-evaluation and initial approval by DCIC, part of the concept is justified by the fact that one fifth of all members' scores are verified by an independent auditor every year. I was now on my way to negotiate a contractual arrangement with the operator of the CSR Database for taking on the task of this independent auditor.

What does one normally associate with the name "auditor"? My mental image is of a dull person, in a dusty suit (and thick glasses!), crunching numbers with an old calculator in a small office. Although my time in a major consultancy had certainly conveyed a more modern picture, this was mostly to do with the suit no longer being dusty, but far more modern. I recognize that this is a caricature, but nevertheless it is still real for me, and here I was about to actively add the title "auditor", even "accountant", to my own identity! One of the reasons I had left the major accountancy-based consulting organization was precisely the falseness I felt was related to the company's own concept of an accountant. Their trust in procedures and checklists to uphold the principles of objectivity and independence contrasted with the many episodes where these principles where subordinated to the need to generate income, almost no matter what. Even though I knew that some of the projects I had undertaken should have been scrutinized and discussed more internally, in order to determine whether they should be taken on in the first place, I hardly ever experienced such a scrutiny from my superiors or those who officially signed declarations of independence and objectivity. Having this in mind certainly colored the way I thought about auditors and accountants in particular.

The meeting with Judy had been set up on the initiative of the former colleague who had developed the CSR Database. Judy did not know very much about third-party verification. As part of the project, my old consulting organization had developed verification guidelines requiring each participating company's own auditors to carry out the verification for CSR Database purposes. I already knew the amount of money set aside for a single verification in the project I was to discuss with Judy, and knew that this was far less than most auditing companies would charge if given the task. In addition, the procedures required DCIC to have their own auditor, who should also be able to give accreditation to other auditors if members wanted to use their own auditor rather than the DCIC one.

Having conducted many verifications, I consider myself a seasoned auditor. Basically, I believe that the conventional accountant approach of number-crunching, systems-checking, limited dialogue and focusing on documentation, is of limited value when applied to CSR. The normal accountant's procedure only scratches the surface and accountants seldom know enough about the subject-matter to provide what I would call meaningful assurance. I regard the normal services provided by accountancy companies to be more or less a smoke-screen for buying a "stamp" of accountability. Auditing companies, on the other hand, will argue that they have abandoned this old-fashioned approach to bring their practice more in line with modern notions of accountability. My own perception of my role as an auditor is more that of an outsider engaging with particular members of a client organization with the purpose of mutual exploration of experiences, sense-making and learning. I believe – but do not know – that I can do something meaningful for the members of CSR Database as their verifier. But along with my general skepticism of the audit business, rooted in the accountancy tradition, another of my concerns about the meeting with Judy was whether the budget constraints for the verification project were too tight to enable much meaningful work to be done.

Getting the job

During my conversation with Judy, I discovered that no one else had been invited to bid for the verification project and that I would not even have to submit a proposal. I knew that it would be difficult for her to find other independent verifiers, particularly given the constraints of the budget. We discussed a possible approach to the verification, and she asked me whether I thought it would be possible to carry this out with the limited money she had available. The project budget allowed for three days' work for each of the selected members, regardless of company size. This would involve at least two meetings; between four and ten interviews, often at different locations; and preparing reports and a verification statement. The sensible thing would have been to say: "No, it is not possible". Nevertheless I said "yes" because the project would boost my cashflow, even if I did have to spend more time than I was being paid for.

Judy informed me that a partner from another major consultancy had been appointed as chair of the Audit Committee. The role of this Audit Committee was to oversee the verification work; this made me feel a little anxious. Naturally Judy had gone for a safe option by putting a well-known partner from another accountancy firm in charge of the Audit Committee, which was to officially guarantee the third-party assessment. This would mean that I would have to document my work according to the standards of accountancy companies. I already knew from internal audits in my previous company that this would entail formal paper trails, including risk assessments, work plans, audit programs, sign-off and evaluation memos. All these needed to be in place to document the independence and objectivity of the verifier and the credibility of the verification. I knew that I would be writing to myself, in that it was most unlikely that the Audit Committee would ever inspect my files. The paperwork served only to add to the administrative overhead and lower my profit margin!

Even if the files were inspected, would this provide any guarantee of my independence and objectivity? No one would compare my evaluations before and after the project, meaning that all the paper trails would be judged retrospectively, at best. And would such a sign-off be a guarantee? From previous experience, I knew that the sign-off was often a formality, with nobody caring to read the documentation anyway. What was most important to the inspection was that the documents were there and that they had been signed. That was their guarantee of independence and objectivity. From my own experience, I knew that some of the documents were even prepared after the event! Furthermore, the documentation itself could easily be falsified or twisted to serve any purpose, which I knew was done on many occasions in risk evaluations. And even the most carefully prepared documentation would never guarantee that the job had been carried out in an objective and independent manner. These were my speculations, which I realized were not shared by the general public. For some reason, accountancy companies are perceived by the public to operate with the required independence and objectivity.

I thus found myself in a situation where, if I wanted to be a verifier of the CSR Database, I would have to demonstrate independence and objectivity to the Audit Committee. This made me feel vulnerable, because I knew that an audit committee would see nothing but myself and my personal integrity; I had no organization or brand to protect me.

My concerns and anxieties were not shared by Judy. Although I did not raise my concerns myself, it was obvious that Judy seemed to take it for granted that I was independent and objective. I believe she attributed this to my previous employment; in her eyes I was an accountant, and accountants are born objective and independent.

Making compromises

After the meeting, I was left with some unanswered questions and many reflections. First of all, I was struck by the lack of rigor and formality that Judy applied before giving me the job. I knew that such things happen, and that as a consultant I should consider myself lucky to avoid all the formalities. All the same, I found it somewhat questionable that the operator of an ethical database did not apply methods that could survive public scrutiny. On the other hand, what she did might be totally defensible, given that I did possess the necessary expert knowledge and experience in the field. My second question was more directed toward my own ethics. Was it ethical of me to accept a project within a framework that I found flawed, within a concept (the CSR Database) that I felt had built-in contradictions, and finally using an audit methodology that I did not entirely believe in? I justified my participation by hypothesizing that the CSR Database could be improved and further developed. If I could contribute to this further development and also provide learning and gain exposure to the participating companies, my involvement with the CSR Database would be worthwhile.

One could argue that both DCIC and I made compromises. Because I needed the income, I acted in apparent conflict with my own opinion, which was, "I do not believe in the CSR Database concept, therefore I should not endorse it by accepting the verification project". My compromise was between my own *values* and my *need* to fill my project pipeline. Although others also had a negative attitude to the CSR Database, I believed that I could rightfully be accused of not being authentic or of being selfish – just doing it for the money. My first reflections were a reaction to what I saw as the perception that others would have of me, and my reaction caused me to create another rationale, to "excuse" myself for making the compromise, and to articulate some ends that could justify my immediate conduct and make sure that it "looked" right. By turning the verification work into a learning experience for the members and by using the audit results to suggest the improvements that I thought would be needed, I could justify the job to myself. I could even – and justly, I thought – argue that by taking it on I could achieve something better than a more orthodox auditor might manage.

In Judy's case, she believed so much in the idea behind the CSR Database that I think just getting it started was her overriding objective, even if the financing was far too limited to warrant its success. Our conversation left no doubt of her enthusiasm and beliefs: she was passionate about the idea. As I saw it, she wanted to do good for society, even without being able to insure that the outcome – the CSR Database – would be a good product. Judy's compromise was between her own desire and political reality, but it was not necessarily a conscious compromise and not necessarily selfish. It was the route to take, given the constraints that she faced; and in her opinion – I assume – it was one step forward of the many to be taken.

Compromise as an enabling constraint

Does it make sense to speak of what took place in the encounter with Judy as a series of compromises? According to the dictionary, what we call *compromise* is either "a settlement of a dispute in which two or more sides agree to accept less than they originally wanted" or "something that somebody accepts because what was wanted is unattainable". In Judy's case, she most likely got less money than she initially wanted and, as is often the case, an "ideal" budget was unattainable. Given that she had put forward a clear proposition with an accompanying budget, then she could be said to have accepted a compromise. But in reality, she would never know what the "ideal" project would be, or whether less money would result in poorer outcomes. In my case I was forced to balance different aspects and consequences of a potential action, but although it might look to out-siders as if I was compromising some of my values, I could also be said to be doing the opposite. Besides the formal verification, I identified learning as a key outcome, with benefits for those involved in the verification process that would make the work meaningful. At the same time I would insure that the work would fulfill the requirements of an Audit Committee. I was thus creating constraints on my actions, namely, that the verification should entail learning and that it should fulfill the requirements of the Audit Committee; and it was these con-straints that enabled me to go on.

I thereby formulated a project design and justification sufficient for me to accept the job. The result of the reflections was not to change the overarching project, but to change the terms of what was required to achieve the outcome. Instead of making a compromise, like accepting the job because of the money while acknowledging that I would rather have said "no", I ended up really wanting to do the project because I believed it could make a difference. But if I had not initially recognized the compromise, then I would probably not have reflected on what I was doing and so might have ended up either refusing, or accepting the project and then carrying it out in a way that would have been in conflict with my beliefs. Recognizing the compromise, and reflecting on it, in a paradoxical way made the compromise disappear by transforming it into an enabling constraint.

This could be equally true of Judy and DCIC. I think she aimed at something intrinsically good, but the reality forced her to accept compromises to make the project fit the reality of the budget. She did not compromise her overall intent to do something good for the consumer, but could not be sure that the actions following the intent were sufficient. She was thus acting into the unknown, but with a clear intent. She was acting in the way she did – I think – because the constraints imposed on her enabled that very action.

In a way, compromising is the way we discover, negotiate and, to some extent, make use of the constraints we continually encounter in all our day-to-day actions and interactions. What is called "compromising" is the process that enables us to move on rather than being blocked. In some cases, we are aware of the compromises we are about to make. However, often we do not know them in advance and only experience them through the process of acting. What we call compromises are thus experienced in the "living present", that is, actions we take in the present on the basis of expectations for the future that arise in accounts of the past (Stacey *et al.*, 2000). Compromises are rationales we create while we are experiencing the constraints on our actions.

Compromise: universal versus contingent views

The usual definition of what we call "compromise" derives from Kantian thinking on ethics. In this view, we are autonomous individuals who make rational decisions based on reflections independent of action and before the action itself. We are weighing the potential consequences of the outcomes and are using these to decide on whether to proceed or not. We reflect and then we act. But by making compromises, we also indicate that we do not do entirely as we would like to. We acknowledge that there might be many solutions, and that not all of them are wrong in themselves. Here we are not helped very much by Kant's first *categorical imperative*, "Act only according to that maxim by which you can at the same time will that it should become a universal law" (Kant and Paton, 1964). What Kantian thinking offers in the situation of a compromise is a boundary around the potential compromises denoting what we cannot accept, rather than what we can. For example, it is easier to agree that stealing is bad than it is to judge certain types of legal business where the more knowing exploit the less knowing.

In the case of accepting the job as a verifier of the CSR Database, a Kantian perspective would be that you should only accept the job if you believe in what you will be doing. But the "believe in" is so particular to the individual that it tends to be a useless statement in itself, offering little guidance to this same individual, because what one person might use as an argument for accepting a job might not be sufficient for another. However, it would also follow, in the Kantian perspective, that if you did not believe in what you were doing, you should not accept the job. Thus it makes more sense to refuse something from Kant's principles than to accept something.

What we call "compromise" might also be viewed from the purely utilitarian perspective of aiming to achieve the greatest good for the greatest number (e.g. see Benn, 1998). From a utilitarian perspective, the moral act is not a private affair. To the contrary, utilitarianism, like Kant's approach, demands an end that can be universal. The utilitarian universal is the general good, the general happiness of the whole community, while Kant finds the universal in a society of autonomous, rational human beings who apply rationality to the form of their acts. Thus the utilitarian and Kantian perspectives both assume that when you face a compromise you ought to try to generalize, to say to yourself: "What would another person do in my place?". The problem with this is that although we do indeed often ask this question, in our reflection this hypothetical "other person" has to be located in the same circumstances as our own, the same special conditions that in the end are only valid for us.

Although we might be tempted to believe that there is a universal answer to our ethical questions, this is very rarely the case. As pointed out by Mead, "Neither of them [i.e. Kantian perspective or utilitarianism] is able to state the end in terms of the object of desire of the individual" (Mead, 1934: 382). As individuals, we are therefore not assisted very much either by Kant or by utilitarianism when we have to choose between different alternatives that are all universally acceptable. According to Mead it is not the *form* of the act, but the *content* of the act, that we should universalize.

> You do have to bring the end into your intention, into your attitude. You can, at every stage of the act, be acting with reference to the end: and you can embody the end in the steps that you are immediately taking. That is the difference between meaning well and having the right intentions. Of course, you cannot have the final result in your early steps of the act, but you can at least state that act in terms of the conditions which you are meeting.
>
> (Mead, 1934: 383)

In the case of my decision to accept the CSR Database job, I focused on the stated end – the third party verification – but also included a further end for the CSR Database itself: that is, companies embracing CSR in a meaningful way so that consumers could look for useful information about products. In the steps I took, I tried to embody an end that I knew from the beginning was not straightforward and which sometimes entailed interests different from my own.

Through this perspective, "compromising" is understood to be a central aspect of our relating to each other. The basis for what we call "compromise" is our own interests; but in the compromise we have to sacrifice what Mead calls the "narrow self", that is, the self that takes only its own interests into account rather than those of all involved. This leads to the development of a larger self, which can be identified with the interests of others and also transforms the basis for what we call compromise from the self to the relation between the self and the others: "The moral problem is one which involves certain conflicting interests. *All of those interests* which are involved in conflict must be considered" (Mead, 1934: 387, italics added).

The problem, however, is that when our own immediate interests come into conflict with others' interests that we may or may not have recognized, we tend to ignore others and take into account only those interests that are immediate. Thus we do not consider *all interests* and, according to Mead, cannot be said to behave ethically. But is this always true? I do not think that there is a clear answer to that. How is it possible to be sure that we really have taken all pertinent interests into account? Surely the term "all" is naively idealistic? What constitutes "all" interests, and does the understanding of this vary from person to person? I think the answer is "yes", and this is exactly why compromising also contains the built-in opportunity for new things to happen. To quote Mead once again: "There is room for mistakes, but mistakes are not sins" (Mead, 1934: 389).

Limitations of a linear time perspective

The original meaning of the word "compromise", namely, that two parties get less than they originally wanted or that one person accepts something because what he/she wanted was unattainable, entails a linear time perspective. To be aware of having made a compromise, we must know in advance what alternative was available. If that alternative was indeed realistic – for example, someone wanted a wall to be painted red while their partner wanted it green, and they gave in because their partner insisted – it would be clear that a compromise had been reached. The person who capitulated would be reminded of this whenever they saw the wall, and might even feel a sense of loss or regret. On the other hand, they might also be surprised to find that they actually like the green. Thus in the very situation where the decision is taken, where the compromise is made, we are able to visualize what the result will be, although we cannot know in advance what feelings we will subsequently experience.

What we call compromise in the everyday understanding of this word entails a conscious reflection in a linear time structure. If used about the past, it tends to serve as a justification or an explanation of an act where there were conflicting views of the desired result. It might even become an excuse: "I was forced to make a compromise!" If used in the present, it tends to describe why we do something different from what we had previously expected to do, and this will typically entail a rationale created by the weighing of pros and cons and an optimal decision. But most situations are far more complex, and we cannot know if what we really wanted was attainable in reality. In the case of me taking on the auditor project for the CSR Database, I will never know what would have happened had I refused to take the project on. Describing the course of events for others, it might look as though I made a compromise; but in what I did and the way I decided to go about it, I myself did not feel that I was compromising. I did not get less than what I wanted, simply because I will never be able to describe exactly what that was.

Rather than using a linear time perspective, what we call compromise could also be seen as interactions that occur in the living present (Stacey *et al.*, 2000), where we act in the present on the basis of expectations for the future that arise in accounts of the past, all in the present. These accounts of the past influence expectations for the future; but the expectations are also simultaneously affecting the accounts of the past. The living present, therefore, has a circular time structure in which the past changes the future and the future simultaneously changes the past, all in the action of the present. From this perspective, what we call compromise could be seen as an enabling constraint that allows us to go forward without being sure of what the future will bring. In other words, being faced with a choice between "a" and "b", we are forced to reflect on our intent and the actions following from that intent; and through the reflection it becomes clear that it is not a choice we are facing, but rather constraints that will affect our actions and the outcome, without necessarily changing the overall intent. Instead of searching for the optimal decision through some rational analysis of pros and cons, this kind of thinking stipulates reflection on the constraints on our actions that we are facing, and how we can act without changing our overall intent. In the case of my decision, I did not list the pros and cons. Instead, I reflected, not only on what the pros and cons were, but also for whom, thereby including the interest of others as well. These reflections helped me shape my actions and desires without losing sight of my overall intent for the CSR Database.

Compromising, understood in this way, is a positive aspect of acting and when done consciously, involving the self, signals a change in the actions leading to an intent, without necessarily changing the overall intent. The ability to compromise then becomes a strength rather than the weakness that is often suggested by ordinary language, for example, referring to someone as "a man of uncompromising nature", meaning a person with perhaps too strong and visible values. In daily life we make compromises all the time, often without recognizing it. Thus, I would conclude that *what is commonly called compromising is the equivalent of the ongoing negotiation and dialogue that we have with others.*

For me, this perspective on what we call compromise throws up some important considerations regarding values in companies and the potential impact if these values are "uncompromising". In the project for the CSR Database it was very important for me that my work lived up not only to my own standards, but also to those of the accountancy profession. Values of independence and objectivity are no doubt an important foundation of these standards. As a verifier of the CSR Database, I would have to demonstrate independence and objectivity. I did this by not taking these two values literally, by "compromising". Rather than taking such values for granted, compromising thus made me reflect on what these values meant to me in the specific actions I was taking. This is contrary to my experience in the consulting organization I used to work for, where I found that the meaning of these values was seldom discussed. This leads me to several questions: Why is it that seemingly important values in the accountancy profession – like objectivity and independence – are beyond discussion? What is the potential impact of this? What role does compromising play in the way we understand our values?

In the following narrative, I will start to explore this further. Using my experiences as an employee in a consultant accountancy firm, I will argue that employees in these companies are neither independent nor objective: where there is no acknowledgment of the conflicts that emerge from an ordinary need to make money and build a career while hoping to remain independent and objective, these values become nebulous and to some extent meaningless. Using accountancy as an example, and drawing on my own experiences with my former employer and the CSR Database project, I will argue that making compromises helps us to pay attention to the things that matter, thereby helping us to take our own values seriously.

Accounting, compromises and cult values

The history of accounting is as old as civilization. Accountants have participated in the development of cities, trade, and the concepts of wealth and numbers. According to Matthews *et al.* (1998) accountants contributed to the development of money and banking, invented double-entry bookkeeping that fuelled the Italian Renaissance, saved many Industrial Revolution inventors and entrepreneurs from bankruptcy, helped develop the confidence in capital markets necessary for western capitalism, and are by many judged to be central to the information revolution that is transforming the global economy. The inventors and the entrepreneurs of the Industrial Revolution, however, were not cost accountants; and those who survived the inevitable depressions recognized that continued success (and avoiding bankruptcy) required accounting expertise. Accountancy introduced a sense of economic reality, making the economic constraints that the business faced transparent for the business owners and managers. Most of this reality arises in a historical perspective, through book-keeping.

Accountants have developed a strong standing in society through the formalization of their services, expressed in the creation of professional associations. For many years, through these associations accountants have managed to create an image of professionals guided by a strong code of ethics. The contributions of professional accountants during the Second World War have especially emphasized this:

> On price regulation committees, over the problems of clothes, food and raw materials rationing, purchase tax, rent control, custodianship of enemy property and the defense finance regulations, the accountant was brought in to act as an impartial arbiter between the licensing authority, the State, and the trader, or the manufacturer. The accountant's task was to prepare returns so that authorities could compute the extent of available supplies. On the fiscal plane the services of the accountant were indispensable to the smooth running of the financial machine. The impartial computation of liability under the excess profit tax, income tax and the national defense contribution ensured that, as much as possible, the burden of war should be covered from current earnings. Profiteering from the miseries of war, if not totally eliminated, was cut down to the minutest proportions, and much of it can be attributed to the untiring efforts of the accountancy profession.
>
> (Stacey, N. A. H., 1954: 191)

The increased complexity of global companies caused a consolidation of the big accountancy companies, which meant that audit services could provide access to further work. Companies and individuals increasingly turned to accountants to help them cope with the growing weight of taxation that resulted from the imposition of a wide range of new taxes. In addition, the audit has provided direct access to the often more lucrative consultancy work which, although dating back at least into the nineteenth century, has grown at an unprecedented rate during the last quarter of a century.

The dilemmas of accounting: objectivity and independence versus income generation

Strong professionalization, however, has had some negative repercussions. Through restricted access to becoming an accountant and by rejecting services not authorized by the professional bodies, accountants became an elite class with the potential for high incomes. Thus, profit maximization for the members became yet another objective aside from professionalization. When I started at my former consultant accounting firm, I was told that, in principle, I could earn as much money as I wanted. Although I knew this was not true, it is an example of a myth that accountancy companies use heavily when trying to attract new employees. What they did not say is that the partner system demands that you first pay your "toll" to the partners above you. They depend on their employees' earning capacity to feed their own high incomes. The rather unrealistic claim of unlimited high earnings is true to the extent that money-making is one of the key criteria for becoming a partner oneself.

Over the last decade, there have been numerous examples of accountancy companies having problems balancing the desire for personal incomes, reflected in the partner structure, with their roles as respected, independent guardians of economic transactions. The professional bodies were originally set up to protect their members, sometimes by discouraging them from pursuing income opportunities that might damage the profession's image. The high income from consultancy services, however, took some of the focus away from the independent auditing business and the big accountancy companies; and as the partners became increasingly dependent on this income, they experienced greater and greater difficulties in maintaining their integrity and independence as they tried to balance the concerns of their clients.

I witnessed this not long after I joined my former company. A key audit client wanted help in carrying out a project that was close to "green-wash": the dissemination of misleading information by an organization to conceal its abuse of the environment, in order to present a positive public image. When we raised this as an issue with our partner-in-charge, rather than confronting the client with this, he looked at the potential for income generation and overruled our concerns. In the official risk evaluation, our concern was not flagged up. Had it been flagged up, the partner in charge of the client would have stopped the project, not necessarily going back to the client to tackle the issue directly, but more likely by refusing personal involvement in the project and letting another advisor carry it out. His major concern would be the risk such a project posed to his own project portfolio. Clearly, the whole culture of this accounting company was one of protecting one's own income streams; our loyalty was (supposed to be) to our partner structure, rather than to the clients or the profession. This also showed up in the way audits were carried out, where every inspection of files and issues was accompanied by an immense volume of documentation, not for the client, but for the partners in charge. The documentation was done in a hierarchical way, from junior accountant to partner-in-charge, the latter having sole authority to sign off on what was referred to as a "high-level memo".

One of the most spectacular examples of the difficulties of balancing integrity and independence with income generation is the case of Enron and Arthur Andersen, where Arthur Andersen was indicted in 2002 for obstruction of justice following the Chapter 11 bankruptcy protection of Enron (Hawkins and Cohen, 2003). The Enron audit business of Arthur Andersen in the year 2000 amounted to $25 million compared to the consulting work of $27 million (Fusaro and Miller, 2002; Hawkins and Cohen, 2003). The Enron case was only one of many instances where audit companies were accused of wrongdoing. Other prominent cases were those of Waste Management, WorldCom, Sunbeam (Fusaro and Miller, 2002). The public reaction to such high-profile cases has been to intensify regulation, which in turn escalates the demand for audit companies to demonstrate independence through increased documentation. The big question is whether such legislation will actually remedy the root causes of the problems, or whether it is just preserving the fantasy of the existence of such a thing as an independent auditor.

Human relating and "self-serving bias"

The auditing business, as well as many other consultancy businesses, are fundamentally based on human relating. In accounting and auditing companies, the more effectively one secures customer satisfaction and repeat sales, the higher one is valued as a professional. Repeat sales, and knowing what the client wants, fundamentally requires an in-depth understanding of the client and good relations with key contacts. "Target meetings" to discuss additional business opportunities from existing clients are regularly held, and an important part of the methodology in these meetings is to map personal relations with key clients. Good client relations – and bad – inevitably affect one's personal career, thereby destroying any notion of being independent.

Post-Enron and Arthur Andersen, Bazerman *et al.* (2002) described some of the mechanisms behind the apparent accountancy errors. The main reason, they claim, is the so-called "self-serving bias", a bias that happens unconsciously and works by distorting the way people interpret information. This is an example of self-serving bias: Armed with the same information, different people reach different conclusions – ones that favor their own interests (Bazerman *et al.*, 2002: 97). In their study, Bazerman *et al.* give numerous examples of how the judgment of consultants is strongly biased toward the interest of their clients. One might argue that the major accounting companies are large enough to absorb the loss of one client, minimizing the urge to please the client. However, an individual accountant's job and career prospects might be dependent on success with specific clients, as was the case in Arthur Andersen. Rather than introducing new regulatory systems, Bazerman *et al.* recommend eliminating incentives that create self-serving biases: for example, reducing the auditor's interest in whether a client is pleased by the results of an audit. But even in the case of one-off audits, one cannot help being affected by the attitude of the persons audited and by one's own need for self-recognition.

The dilemmas tend to disappear

Although legislation has forced many accountancy companies to reconsider the balance between consulting and accounting practices, many companies outside the US, including Denmark, are strong advocates of keeping consultancy and auditing within one firm. Cross-selling is still a focus area, and the powerful position of key account manager can be attained only by senior managers or partners. Employees in these companies are consequently forced to compromise constantly between the need to be independent and objective while at the same time creating strong bonds with the client and focusing on increased cross-selling. But as long as these compromises are not named or acknowledged, then they are not seen to exist within the company.

The apparent paradox – needing to be independent and objective while at the same time developing strong relations with those who, in principle, should not influence one's practice – is resolved in several ways. One way is by applying a linear time perspective, by relating with the client in the phases leading up to a project, then retrospectively demonstrating independence in carrying out the project. Another is through self-deception, by defining independence solely in terms of economic interests. All internal procedures for proving independence, therefore, deal only with potential financial conflicts of interest with the client, and not with any kind of personal relations that may exist. Independence thereby becomes an attribute of an object, rather than a relation in itself.

In the various kinds of auditing that I have been involved in, it is clear that audits evolving from the tradition of accountancy companies tend to avoid extensive interaction with the clients. Instead, the auditing process focuses on numbers and systems. This focus, the preservation of an outside perspective and establishing a temporary existence as controllers in separate on-the-premises offices, maintains the perception of being independent and contributes to the self-deception already mentioned. Consequently the perception that accountancy companies, through their design of certain tasks and values, are independent and objective, appears to me to be nothing but an illusion upheld by the companies themselves. This illusion has permeated society to a considerable extent, and in the case of the CSR Database the fact that I had been employed by an accountancy company and thus knew about audit methodologies was enough to credit me with the independence and objectivity needed for the job. I was very much aware of the so called "self-serving bias" of consultancy work, and knew that I had to think of independence and objectivity in a different way when actually carrying out the verification work itself. This different understanding is fundamental for the type of audit work I do concerning assurance and accountability. Why, then, is it so difficult for accountancy companies to acknowledge the problems related to independency and objectivity? Part of this – I believe – has to do with the strong reliance of the accountancy profession on systems theory, which I will discuss in the next section.

Accounting, auditing and systems theory

General audit principles have remained unchanged through history. Auditors are supposed to be independent, to be objective in their observations, with a duty to report their findings. Although accounting and auditing in principle are older than systems theory, which as a general theory first commanded widespread attention after World War II (Jackson, 2000), these general audit principles fit very well with systems thinking. The audit object is considered to be a "thing", a system, which the auditor can objectively observe and evaluate. With the introduction, in the 1980s, of various management systems for quality assurance, environmental protection and other related issues, it became increasingly clear just how much accounting and auditing relied on systems thinking. The remit of auditors is to check the implementation of these various systems; not only is it their intention to check the internal controls and feedback systems, but the auditing itself can also be regarded as a control system. With the widespread growth of issue-specific management systems, there has been a surge toward the integration of management systems. This has spurred the development of more integrated approaches to auditing, inspired not only by systems theory and focusing on interdependencies within the company systems (Karapetrovic and Willborn, 2000), but also by Senge's Learning Organization (Beckett and Murray, 2000). This development has led to a confirmation of auditing as firmly rooted in systems theory.

It seems natural that a profession that is in essence about systems checking must itself be based on systems thinking. Consequently, the basis for accounting and auditing firms is their own systems and procedures, which are applied in auditing routines to insure objectivity in the reporting of findings. Auditing firms typically have strict hierarchical organizational forms, with very precise descriptions of function and authority (Hawkins and Cohen, 2003). These firms also have procedures for judging the principle of independence. This principle, which is fundamentally linked to the principle of objectivity, is the Achilles' heel of the accountant and auditing firms. Compromising is not an issue, because in principle an optimal solution can always be found through rational thinking. Again, the belief in the accounting methodologies is so strong that the accountancy companies themselves have little doubt that they can be applied to areas other than economics, for example, the environment and CSR.

These systems thinking-based methodologies are presented by the companies as a guarantee of trustworthiness and, when combined with the brand of objectivity and independence, are often accepted at face value by others who need to demonstrate accountability, as in the case of the CSR Database. Ideals rooted in values like objectivity and independence are not bad in themselves; in fact, one would think that building a company on these values would foster something good. The problem, however, is that there are other ideals in play at the same time, which have developed and become an important part of most accountancy company ideals, and these have come to work against objectivity and independence. It is to these issues that I will now turn.

Accounting, ideals and compromises

The original ideal for accountancy companies was linked to the three principles of being *independent*, *objective*, and with *a duty to report findings* (Karapetrovic and Willborn, 2000). In this way, accountants are the guardians of the financial system, giving trust to financial operations and investments. Apart from this ideal, employees in accountancy companies aspire to become successful (and rich) partners. The successful partner is a role model held up for the employees and in this way also a kind of ideal, although of a different character. While the first one is rooted in idealism, that is, a theory positing the primacy of spirit, mind, or language over matter, the latter is driven by materialism and pragmatism, a tendency that seems to become more and more prevalent in today's society. These two contrasting ideals often work in the same direction. Being good at the primary task of the accountant means being recognized for one's efforts and skills, resulting in gradual progress up the ladder that culminates in becoming a partner.

The road toward partner status is long and burdensome, and the temptation to make short-cuts by uncritically securing new projects rather than upholding the strictest accountancy ideals is a daily challenge. Usually, this involves minor decisions and actions where the need for income is placed above accountancy principles. While claiming to uphold the ideal of an independent and objective accountant, one can demonstrate that in some cases this ideal can be compromised in the interests of securing a new project or opportunity on behalf of the company. This was what I experienced in my former company: whenever new project opportunities were few, what mattered was an individual's ability to generate income; anyone who lacked this ability risked being squeezed out of the company. Business opportunities, job security and the ideal of the successful partner thereby become more important than the ideal of accountancy.

The compromise we make in this case is not necessarily paradoxical, because we resolve it by ranking our ideals. Furthermore, our actions are very often unconscious. We might not even be aware of what we are doing because it has become part of the day-to-day practice; it has been accepted because superiors stress the need for income and never question the accountancy ideals. Rather, these ideals are taken for granted. Only when many small actions combine to make our doings visible to others do we realize that we have done something that is not laudable. In some cases this "something" might even be a violation of laws or internal rules. Similarly, an auditor's biases may lead them to unknowingly adapt over time to small imperfections in a client's financial practices. Eventually, though, the sum of these small judgments may become sufficiently large that the long-standing bias becomes apparent. At that point, correcting the bias may require admitting prior errors. Rather than expose the unwitting mistakes, the auditor may decide to conceal the problem. Thus, unconscious bias may evolve into conscious corruption – corruption representing the most visible end to a situation that may have been deteriorating for some time: "It's our belief that some of the recent financial disasters we've witnessed began as minor errors of judgment and escalated into corruption" (Bazerman *et al.*, 2002: 101).

Contemporary role models

Often, when we use the phrase *being ethical*, we speak of being true to our ideals. Ideals here can be anything from philosophical ideals to role models. The role models used to be extraordinary people embodying philosophical ideals. In modern times, our role models have changed dramatically from being people who embody philosophical ideals to people who achieve personal success in the form of fame and power. The enormous influence of the media has even spurred the development of ideals whose role models' only attribute is that they are famous – the cult of the celebrity. Our ideals have thus changed from being unattainable and utopian to more pragmatic goals attainable by everyone, taking the form of self-fulfillment, of "being true to ourselves" (Taylor, 1991; Bloom, 1987). This need for self-fulfillment has led to the development of a kind of "value-abundant" society where everyone has his or her own "values" and where is it illegitimate to challenge another's values (Bloom, 1987). According to Taylor the problem, however, is not the ideal of authenticity in itself but the risk that individualism causes one to lose a sense of a bigger purpose, leading to a flattened and narrower life. This is linked to the widespread use of "instrumental reason", that is, the kind of rationality we draw on when we calculate the most economic application of means to a given end (Taylor, 1991). Authentically being true to oneself, according to Taylor, means finding one's own originality, which is something we can discover only in a dialogical process. Defining oneself means finding what is significantly different from others; but finding the difference is not just a matter of choice. It has to be a choice that recognizes other issues of significance apart from the choice itself:

> The agent seeking significance in life, trying to define him- or herself meaningfully, has to exist in a horizon of important questions. That is what is self-defeating in modes of contemporary culture that concentrate on self-fulfillment in opposition to the demands of society, or nature, which shut out history and the bonds of solidarity.
>
> (Taylor, 1991: 40)

My ideal

My ideal, at the time I worked for an accountancy firm, evolved around personal integrity and my role model was especially my former boss. At the same time, I saw wealth, formal position and the ability to make money as important tokens of success, although I recognized that they often conflicted with personal integrity. My attraction to my former company was to work with an international company, where I assumed that integrity would be a key value, and to sustain a relatively high income. I was told that I was to be positioned for a fast-track partner admission. I soon found, however, that although integrity was certainly a featured value in the glossy brochures about the company, it did not penetrate very deep. Promises and personal integrity seemed to come second to income generation. If we did not bring in sufficient money, the promises made to us were abandoned, and if we had the chance to generate money we could bend our integrity to serve this purpose.

It was not always pleasant to be confronted with many "successful" partners who were good at making money but were not very bright and did not demonstrate much integrity. I soon lost whatever might have been left of the idea that integrity was a prerequisite to earning tokens of success, such as formal position and recognition. I increasingly realized that money had played too big a role in my choice to join the company and that I had neglected other issues of significance. While I gradually experienced and recognized the downsides of the company, I also gradually realized how I had become part of the downside. In order to have a say, it was essential to aim for partner status oneself, and in order to become a partner the most important criterion was to generate income. Instead of being true to my own ideals by considering the question of integrity, I was gradually destroying my ideals, at the cost of my own identity. Part of this identity, I realize, was also connected to the values of objectivity and independence that I can easily trace back to my initial interest in rationality and science. I was faced with the fact that the company which, in principle, should embody these values now seemed to destroy them for me.

What about other employees in that company? Can they maintain values of objectivity and independence? I do not believe so, because any problems related to these values remain unacknowledged and are not openly discussed in the organization. This and the conflicting ideals, I think, are some of the reasons that prevent the elimination of what I call the illusion of objectivity and independence of accountancy companies. In the next section I will look more closely at the way values are interpreted, or not interpreted, in the daily practice of an accountancy company and how this can eventually lead to a culture that works against these same values. I will contrast this with my experiences from the CSR Database project, which I undertook as a self-employed person.

Cult values and functionalization

George Herbert Mead, the American pragmatist and social psychologist, offers several insights into the genesis of values and the development of what he called a *cult*. In his terminology, values such as becoming rich and powerful can be said to be the result of an idealization of the collective of powerful partners (Mead, 1934, 1964). He called these *cult values*. In Mead's understanding, all values – positive as well as negative – are cult values. Mead also defines what he calls a *functional value*, which is the way a cult value is functionalized in our everyday actions. Such a functionalization inevitably causes conflicts because there is no unique functionalization. These conflicts then have to be negotiated between people in their practical interactions with each other, leading to a consolidated understanding of the cult value and the possibility for changes in the way the cult values are understood. If you apply the cult values directly without functionalization, they tend to become overriding universal norms to which members must conform. Such memberships constitute what we normally understand to be a *cult*. The functionalization of the cult value of becoming rich and powerful takes the form of a variety of ways of making money, often disregarding other ideals or seriously infringing them. Such cult values thus tend to make it more important for employees to think about how to make money than to think about the way money is made, thereby diverting their attention from the ethics of their daily actions (Griffin, 2002).

The conflict between the cult values of independence and objectivity and those rooted in the wealthy and powerful partner ideal is very seldom addressed in daily practice. Formally, it is recognized and dealt with in various procedures before starting a new project, which each person who is assigned an overall project responsibility must adhere to. Basically, the auditor must complete a risk assessment evaluating their own competence and independence. Usually what this means is that one cannot both audit and consult to the same client at the same time, although this is not always adhered to. The key procedure to demonstrate independence is the yearly declaration of financial independence of the clients. The procedures outline some general rules that must be followed, but apart from these they are regarded as formalities. By this means, the ideals of independence and objectivity in daily practice are subjugated to the application of rational procedures, and being a good accountant becomes synonymous with the ability to make money. Unless able to demonstrate this ability, one has a limited future in the company and definitely no partner potential. On the other hand, it is possible to become a partner without demonstrating the ideals of independence and objectivity, because it is tacitly assumed that these are fundamental prerequisites of being a successful professional. This illustrates the core problem: independence is implicitly assumed to be inseparable from winning clients, instead of being inherently at odds with consistently sustaining and expanding the client base.

This is another example of the abundant use of Charles Taylor's "instrumental reasoning". Management do not pay attention to the potential conflicts in the functionalization of the various cult values, and ignore/are not aware of the potential bad practices that unwittingly may have evolved. Instead they have idealized the non-conflict between the different cult values and created a third cult value: that is, independence and objectivity are assured by the absence of direct financial interest in the client company. This cult value is applied directly through the procedures and criteria that explicitly define "direct financial interest", and is never really functionalized. Thereby, employees are freed of the conflicts that normally arise in functionalization and any compromise that they might think they could face; that is, the compromise is made purely hypothetical. Instead, what matters is that the required documentation is in place – that is, the relevant procedures and checklists are in place and will be available for internal inspection. Although from time to time one might question whether one is truly independent and objective, the fact that the necessary documentation has been applied exempts one from paying attention to the potential conflicts of interest that might arise when actually carrying out the project. In this way it is both a smokescreen and a false security, caused by the heavy reliance on systems thinking and the linear time perspective applied.

In the CSR Database project, I knew I had to demonstrate to the Audit Committee that I had procedures and documentation in place. For each of the ten audits I prepared a letter of engagement, an audit plan, a risk assessment, a planning memo, documentation of interviews, a declaration and a post-project memo. I knew that this formed the backbone of the evidence required for the Audit Committee that the verification had been conducted to the best professional standards. At the same time, I realized that to do a good job I needed to relate to the clients, and I needed to make many assumptions and personal evaluations. So I was not independent and could not be objective in the conventional/literal meaning of these words. The "objectivity" applied in the verification and my "independence" had to rely on my judgment and the personal integrity I invested in all the verifications, however fragile that may be. I thus had to functionalize the principles of objectivity and independence faced with the dilemmas and conflicts of carrying out the project. I was compromising. But I did it consciously and not against my ideal. Compromising thereby became the very way I came to make sense of the principles of "objectivity" and "independency", and helped me pay attention to what was important for me. This not only made it meaningful for me to conduct the verification, but also meant that these two principles could become part of my values.

In my former company, this could never have happened because the two principles were "uncompromisable" and not open for discussion. By not acknowledging the problems related to this non-functionalization of cult values, accountancy companies risk developing a cult with their own understanding of what independence and objectivity mean. Employees then become part of an *enlarged personality* (Stacey, 2003), where there is no need to consider what objectivity and independency mean. As a member of a cult, one's identity will inevitably become affected by this.

Strong and weak evaluations

So far, I have claimed that making a compromise does not necessarily mean going against one's ideals. One is functionalizing the values making up the ideal. The argument could be made, however, that one can go against your ideals, and when one does this it is making a compromise. We know what we think would be the right thing to do, but the circumstances make us take a deliberate decision to act differently. This kind of compromise is, in my opinion, based on what I earlier called rational, linear thinking. We are considering pros and cons, and end up in a compromise that is rationally defendable.

This is the kind of rationalism that is also the basis of "economical reasoning" defined by Charles Taylor, which is partially the cause of many "false" ideals (Taylor, 1991). These kinds of rational decisions presume that we know the potential outcome of our actions. They are fundamental to systems thinking and rely on the kind of rationality that is used in traditional science, where we aim to find the objective truth. This kind of rationality leads us to think that we can predict the future and leads us to define criteria for success that can guide us in our decisions. Ideally, this rationality also dissolves the compromise because in theory we should be able to find the optimal solution.

When we nevertheless feel that we have been making a compromise, it is exactly because feelings have been excluded from this rational decision-making. We have transformed what Charles Taylor names a *strong evaluation*, which is when we reject a perfectly realizable desire because we believe it is unacceptable, into what he calls a *weak evaluation* (Taylor, 1989) by the use of rationality. According to Taylor, a *weak evaluation* is the criterion we use to choose between two conflicting desires, where the conflict is a practical matter, so it is not possible to realize both of them in a particular, limiting situation.

A weak evaluation is thus very similar to the ordinary understanding of a compromise. What happens is that we discard our ideals by rationalization, by neglecting or overruling our feelings, and turn the situation into a choice between conflicting desires, only one of which is practically possible. We thereby avoid strong evaluations and risk a loss of identity. Acknowledging these feelings and paying attention to them could help us to become clearer about our ideals and about the necessary functionalization of the cult values.

Richard Rorty (1991) suggests that there is another kind of rationality. In his sense the word "rational" means something like "sane" or "reasonable" rather than "methodical".

> It then comes to encompass a set of moral virtues like tolerance, respect for the opinions of those around one, willingness to listen, reliance on persuasion rather than force.
>
> (Rorty, 1991: 37)

This kind of rationality comes closer to the kind of critical reflection that is necessary when we engage in the conflicting processes of functionalization than the rationality we apply in the weak evaluations that Taylor discusses. Applying Rorty's notion of rationality could even show us a totally new way of understanding our own ideals. Using the kind of rationality championed by Rorty, in my view, helps us make the compromises that will prevent our ideals from becoming simply put and non-functionalizable. Being able to compromise in this respect becomes a real individual asset, in relation to which the apparently positive assertion, "an uncompromising nature", should be regarded as something less favorable.

References

Bazerman, M. H., Loewenstein, G. and Moore, D. A. (2002) "Why good accountants do bad audits", *Harvard Business Review*, 80 (11): 96–102.

Beckett, R. and Murray, P. (2000) "Learning by auditing: A knowledge creating approach", *The TQM Magazine*, 12: 125–36.

Benn, P. (1998) *Ethics*, Montreal, London, Buffalo: McGill-Queen's University Press.

Bloom, A. D. (1987) *The Closing of the American Mind*, New York: Simon and Schuster.

Fusaro, P. C. and Miller, R. M. (2002) *What Went Wrong at Enron: Everyone's Guide to the Largest Bankruptcy in U.S. History*, Hoboken, NJ: J. Wiley.

Griffin, D. (2002) *The Emergence of Leadership: Linking Self-organization and Ethics*, New York and London: Routledge.

Hawkins, D. F. and Cohen, J. (2003) "Arthur Andersen LLP", *Harvard Business School*, Case Study 9–103–061.

Investopedia.com (2005) Sarbanes–Oxley Act of 2002 – SOX. www.investopedia.com.

Jackson, M. C. (2000) *Systems Approaches to Management*, New York: Kluwer.

Kant, I. (1964) *Groundwork of the Metaphysic of Morals*, New York: Harper & Row.

Karapetrovic, S. and Willborn, W. (2000) "Generic audit of management systems: fundamentals", *Managerial Auditing Journal*, 15, 6: 279–94.

Matthews, D., Anderson, M. and Edwards, J. R. (1998) *The Priesthood of Industry: The Rise of the Professional Accountant in British Management*, Oxford: Oxford University Press.

Mead, G. H. (1964) in Reck, A. J. (ed.) *Selected Writings*, Indianapolis: Bobbs-Merrill.

Mead, G. H. (1934) in Morris, C. W. (ed.) *Mind, Self, and Society: From the Standpoint of a Social Behaviorist*, Chicago: University of Chicago Press.

Rorty, R. (1991) *Objectivity, Relativism, and Truth*, Cambridge and New York: Cambridge University Press.

Stacey, N. A. H. (1954) *English Accountancy: A Study in Social and Economic History, 1800–1954*, London: Gee.

Stacey, R. D. (2003) 4th ed. *Strategic Management and Organisational Dynamics: The Challenge of Complexity*, Harlow: Financial Times Prentice Hall.

Stacey, R. D., Griffin, D. and Shaw, P. (2000) *Complexity and Management: Fad or Radical Challenge to Systems Thinking?*, New York: Routledge.

Taylor, C. (1989) *Sources of the Self: The Making of the Modern Identity*, Cambridge, MA: Harvard University Press.

Taylor, C. (1991) *The Ethics of Authenticity*, Cambridge, MA: Harvard University Press.

Editors' introduction to Chapter 5

For some time now, those engaging in the activity of leading in changing, learning organizations, as well as those writing about such activities, have made strong links between effective leadership and a leader's capacity for self-mastery, based on values. Some influential writers have also coupled notions of self-mastery with various forms of spirituality in which the self-mastery of the individual leader is understood to amount to a process of self-transcendence, involving identification with, even submission to, a greater purpose and transcendent "whole". Such self-mastery is sometimes described as "ruthless compassion". However, notions of self-mastery and ruthless compassion are generally described in rather harmonious, even mystical terms. It is rare to find explorations of just what it actually means to master oneself and the pain that this might involve. It is even rarer to find explorations of just what it actually means to be ruthless as in ruthless compassion. The leadership literature does not deal much at all with the need leaders often experience to take ruthless actions.

The author of this chapter, Martin Daly, is the principal of a school. The story he tells in this chapter is about the ruthless action he felt compelled to take to remove a non-performing teacher from his school. The actions he took eventually led to legal action against him and his school and this received considerable media coverage in which, at first, he was vilified. It is in this context that he explores what "ruthless compassion" and "self-mastery" mean to him. Central themes in his exploration have to do with what it means to act with intention in such circumstances and how intertwined such intention is with value commitment. He writes about the intentional, value-driven refusal to compromise. Previous chapters in this volume have focused attention on values, the inevitable conflict that arises when the idealizations of value are made functional in contingent situations and the compromises this so often entails. This chapter focuses our attention on how and why the commitment to value may actually call for a "no compromise" response. However, Daly argues that the ethical "no compromise" response demands as rigorously reflexive an attitude as the kind of ethical compromise Drabæk wrote about in the last chapter.

Daly argues that the self-mastery required for ethically making a "no compromise" response is the result of the painful, hard work of self-examination to empty oneself of the desire to crush, seek revenge, intimidate or provoke others, as well as attendant feelings of frustration, anger and omnipotence. He describes this as the achievement of a position of detached involvement in which desires and feelings not connected to the organizational task have been stripped away. Daly takes issue with Senge's view of the learning organizational discipline of personal mastery required of effective leaders because it omits the pain, struggle, self emptying, even death of self that such mastery requires. He is also critical of Senge's importation of religious language into a secular setting without grounding it in the everyday work experience of managers. He asks how one is supposed to evaluate the difference between a self-mastering leader, a deeply convinced fanatic or an arrogant bully.

Daly concludes the chapter with a discussion of the origin of values, comparing a pragmatic view of value as emerging in interactive experience between people in contingent situations and a metaphysical view of values as absolutes given to us. He is not satisfied with taking up either of these positions to the exclusion of the other because, for him, this would lose the paradox of the everyday and the metaphysical, of freedom and obedience, autonomy and submission.

5 Leadership and self-mastery

Values and the "no compromise" response

Martin Daly

This chapter is structured around a narrative of what took place at an employment appeals tribunal involving a member of staff at the school of which I am principal. It is part of a much more extensive narrative of how I take up my role in relation to all the school's stakeholders including the staff. The events in which I have been involved have led me to examine what leading has demanded of me: a struggle to control and master myself. This notion is taken up in Peter Senge's books, *The Fifth Discipline* and *Presence*. In reflecting on what motivates me to struggle with myself, I draw on Charles Taylor's and Alasdair MacIntyre's work on the ground of values. In conjunction with the theme of self-mastery and control, I would like to investigate what I mean by intention, where I think it comes from and how it stays the same/changes over time. Does intention arise in action as the pragmatist position would hold? Or does the source of my intention lie in some metaphysical realm? I want to begin to think through some of the assumptions about intention that inform the stories I live and tell in my practice and to examine some of the questions my involvement as principal in an institution akin to many other public service institutions raises.

My experience as principal for many years and as a consultant to principals and to a number of CEOs in the public services, has been that many managers are at a loss as to how to act in such settings due to the fact that the roles, relationships, work practices and conditions of employment are set in stone. In particular, there are many situations where the security of tenure enjoyed by staff means that regardless of how the service delivers on what it is supposed to deliver, it rarely has any implications for members of staff. When this is coupled with a highly unionized environment, entrenched work practices and an antipathy toward any exercise of authority or attempt to introduce systems of appraisal, the role of the manager is extremely challenging. How, for example, is one to introduce any internal accountability in such situations? Any taking of authority risks being labeled hierarchical and a form of bullying. In my opinion, the most critical issue at the present time across the public services and institutions involved in providing such services, is how managers are to take up authority and exercise leadership on behalf of the service as a whole.

Retelling stories

Jeanette Winterson once said that she wrote in order to have something to read. I remembered her comment as soon as I began to write this paper because of my own need to write and rewrite, to read and reread, what I had written. I have spent many hours recounting this story to myself and others as it developed. I have never told the same version twice. The story is forever moving. Retelling it in this chapter is not a further ossification of the dead bones of a particular episode, but an attempt in doing so to change my relationship to what happened in the hope that this will enable me to think in a richer and more nuanced manner that may engender greater flexibility in the future.

Relating theory and experience in writing

In making available and using my experience as a manager in this way, I consider my practice as always potential research. One of the lacunae in much management research is that it is unrelated to people's experience of managing (MacLean, 2004). The starting point for this piece of research is my experience of intense involvement in managing a particularly difficult situation over a lengthy period of time. Out of that involvement, I engage with literature that provides more or less enriching interpretations of that experience. This engagement with the literature feels like another dimension of my involvement as a manager – not an activity on some more abstract level.

I consider that my primary responsibility as a manager is to be reflexive within my interactions with others, i.e. to be mindful of my contribution to the worlds of meaning that are being generated. "Conversation takes on a moral dimension because through this medium managers are positioned to facilitate or inhibit powers for self and others to act" (Oliver, 2002: 5). This chapter describes how I made things happen and how things happened that made my responses. It also inquires into the how of that how: how did I "make" myself in making things happen and how was I unmade and remade in doing so. It inquires and critiques how recent writers describe this process.

I was appointed Principal of a boys' school a number of years ago. The school is owned and run by a religious order. In my time in the school, its reputation has risen dramatically. I have instigated changes in every area of the school's life, but particularly in how staff are managed. The school has always been known for the quality of the relationships between all parties. In the past, the atmosphere would have been described by members of the order and by the staff as familial, like a home away from home, where we were all "in it" together. Part of the folklore of the school is that it was described years ago by a principal as having a certain "indefinable quality", a certain "je ne sais quoi". It was more than a business or a place for achieving high exam grades, but a Christian community, concerned with the formation of the hearts, minds and souls of the pupils. The principal was regarded as a pastoral paternal spiritual leader. Evaluation of exam results, for example, would have been regarded as unseemly. It just wasn't done. Historically, the management style had been a mix of autocracy and charisma combined with a laissez-faire approach to everyday matters. The school was ruled from on high, but on the ground there were very few checks going on about any aspect of the work.

I had been a member of staff for a number of years prior to being appointed as principal. I felt that while people were very positive about my appointment, there was a sense that as I had been one of the staff, I would remain so even as principal. At the first staff meeting I endeavored to set out a context for my transition from being a member of staff to my being principal In particular, I spoke about the need to be professional and how I would try not to personalize issues that arose between us. I wanted to reassure the staff of my intention to relate to them fairly, in a manner that they could rely on. I meant to increase their sense of safety. The staff did not perhaps fully realize what I intended when I made that distinction. If the truth were told, I don't know if I did either. In hindsight, the seeds of destruction "of the way things were done" were present in genesis in that distinction. I signaled a new way of relating.

I might have added: "I also expect you to be professional in your relationships with me especially when I take a decision with which you disagree". As I write this now I realize that I, albeit inchoately, wanted to signal something else that I knew would happen. Or is that just hindsight? I felt from the first day that the staff would feel betrayed by me. I did not consciously intend on the first day to betray them. I was hoping – naively I admit – that making such a distinction would be enough for people to remember when the crunch came that I was only doing my job. However, as time went on, I found myself interpreting what it meant to be professional not personal in a way that I had not worked out in the beginning though I felt as I went on that I had known it all along.

The distinction between the personal and the professional, only took on a meaning in the moment. How can actions not be "personalized", but be seen as professional when they have very personal consequences for others' lives and split the staff down the middle? I never envisaged that things would get to that point. When they did, I wanted, even in those moments, for the staff not to personalize what was happening. I wanted to scream at them: "Now do you see what I mean? What do you think I was talking about all along? If I can desist from personalizing it and I am the one in the line of fire, why can't you do the same?" When I say that I distinguished the personal from the professional, in another way I personalized and inter-personalized everything. I focused my attention on the professional people and I put all of my energy into addressing issues of professionalism with them.

Reflection on the nature of intention

Did I know from the start what I intended or did the intention only arise in the course of my involved everyday coping with being principal?

Griffin (2002: 15) identifies, as the very essence of experience, that thought does not arise before action, but that in the ongoing dynamic interaction between thought and action, meaning is being made and remade. In arriving at this position he explains how Kant introduced the "both ... and" way of thinking about causation and time, whereby human beings are both subject to the laws of nature and retain their freedom to set their own purposes, in my words, to decide their intentions, as they are able to understand nature from the position of objective detached observers.

According to Kant, to be human is to set goals for our actions, but we can think about nature as if it had goals, that is, nature can be seen as a system that unfolds what is enfolded within itself, realizing the potential contained in seed form initially. Human freedom is retained because the human being is the one thinking of nature as if its parts were organized to produce a particular whole. He or she puts notions of intention, goals and purposes "into" the system of nature "as if" they were there in embryo.

Griffin argues that we have come to think of organizations in the same way and that this is contrary to Kant's intention in proposing this structure: he maintained that such thinking could not be applied to human action. When this structure is applied to managers in what Griffin calls "systemic self-organization", they are positioned as standing outside the system of the organization acting on it, inputting their intentions, responsible for shaping and controlling the system while the system in which we all participate is seen as self-organizing, having a purpose all of its own which it itself intends and to which we are subject, and so we speak of the "organization" or the "school" as if it existed independently of our participation in creating it. Instead, Griffin argues that at one and the same time, we are forming and being formed in the process of interaction with each other, in what he calls "participative self-organization". This process has its own purpose, "namely, the process of constructing the as yet unknown future. Such a process is understood as transforming itself from within" (ibid.: 14). We cannot know the outcome of actions before they occur. Our intentions arise prior to rather than within the action. Neither description of self-organization on its own fits with my everyday experience of having to manage. My experience is that I both had a prior intention as to what I wanted to achieve and how I wanted to achieve it and that the intention moved/evolved in response to what happened on a moment to moment basis. This position echoes MacIntyre's (1981) notion of a "quest" wherein both unpredictability and the idea of a telos or goal are included. Both positions feel true when taken together, but only partially true when taken separately.

I hold that my future intentions were present embryonically in that initial declaration at the staff meeting and that what I intended had to be interpreted, negotiated and fleshed out as I interacted with others. In hindsight, I would feel that my actions in relation to the members of staff in the narrative below are recognizable as the working out in a concrete situation of what I intended. At the same time, I could not have told anyone at the beginning what it might involve in the concrete and my intention only came into existence in the concrete situation.

It seems to me that intention has a known/unknown quality to it. Charles Taylor, drawing on Merleau-Ponty's (1962) account of being-devoted-to-the-world and Heidegger's (1962) being-in-the-world, argues that we directly get to grips with the things and people that make up our world. We are first of all immediately and spontaneously involved in coping with the world, making our way in it. This is pre-conceptual. The notion of a pre-reflective grip or grasp of knowledge suggests to me some sense of intention being pre-conceptual, not thought out, but known as I am involved in acting. In my case, I know that I had a very strong, albeit unarticulated, sense of my intention. I knew without conceptualizing it what I was about and what I wanted to do. I am first involved in coping with a world that lays claim on me to do so and I respond spontaneously and pre-conceptually to what it throws at me and evokes in me. I felt addressed by the situation I describe below that called forth in me spontaneous responses that fleshed out what I on a pre-reflective level intended. Something in the notion of a pre-reflective grasp, captures the pre-conceptual yet real existence of my intention and describes my experience of managing-in-the-school.

Continuation of the narrative

As I tell the story of what took place and offer some reflections on it, I particularly want to track the movement of my intention. I recall a conversation with the Deputy Principal soon after I was appointed as Principal. She said that the critical issue in the school that had to be addressed was the quality of teaching and learning and that in this regard the performance of teachers individually in their subjects and collectively in their departments had to be reviewed. However, she was skeptical that anything much could be done and did not know how to go about initiating such a review. The conversation stayed with me. I was of the same opinion as she was, but I did not share her lack of hope. I notice how I am always drawn to situations that are apparently intractable or taken for granted and want to provoke change. I am most interested in the challenge of creating movement out of such stuckness.

I felt I had an insider's knowledge of the situation having taught in the school for a number of years prior to becoming principal and had worked closely with my predecessor. I set out with the intention of addressing every and any issue that I felt was critical to the well-being of the school and to deal head on with any issue that arose in doing so, whatever that might involve. I acknowledge that my experience as a teacher had prejudiced me in regard to staff both positively and negatively, but I hoped – naively perhaps – that if I was consistently "upfront" with everyone in regard to what I expected and how I felt they were performing, then ultimately they would respond. I realize now that my intention was, as I said at the first staff meeting, "to engage constructively with staff around the task of the school". That constructive engagement was both my means and hoped-for end, my process and desired product. I thought that if I could eliminate or greatly reduce the "anti-task" behavior of which I was aware, we could all then get on with the real work of the school. I realize in hindsight that I did not see the "real work" as the negotiation with the staff about what the task actually is. I did realize even then that this would inevitably lead to conflict. I just did not and could not have foreseen what it would demand of me and of others. Now, I am more inclined to see how each of us displays both elements of pro- and anti-task behavior at the same time and that defining the "task" is a matter of ongoing negotiation. I assumed that once negotiated, and once clarity of roles and responsibilities was achieved, we could move on and the messiness of negotiating would diminish.

I had other assumptions that betrayed themselves to me as time went on. I assumed that I was not part of this messiness, that I was not displaying any of what I termed "anti-task" behavior, and so I located it in others. Thus, I assumed that tackling the problem meant primarily dealing with individuals. I saw myself as acting "on" the system as a whole and on the individual parts to change it along the lines of the systemic self-organization model to which I referred earlier.

How was my intention formed?

There was an intention, but the meat was put on the bones of this intention as I began to get involved in particular interactions. This is where the Kantian notion of unfolding of what was enfolded within the system makes partial sense of my experience. In hindsight, the manner in which I tackled all areas of the school is consistent with the initial acorn of motivation that I felt from that conversation with the deputy principal. I regarded every interaction as potentially a strategic event and I was hyper-vigilant. I grasped that I was influencing and being influenced every time I talked with someone, negotiating "how things were done". In that negotiating, I was participating in the ongoing creation of intention and purpose with the staff. Every minute patterning was also patterning the whole school relationships in the moment. Nobody had to tell me that: I knew it innately. I recognized what I knew already. My experience of learning is of recognizing explicitly on reflection what on a pre-reflective level, I have already grasped.

We began to meet a number of staff who were either experiencing difficulties in class and/or about whom we were hearing complaints from parents and pupils. We decided that when doing so, any significant conversation with any other teacher would be minuted and a copy of our minutes of the meeting would be given to the person. In doing so, we were consciously formalizing the conversations with staff. This formalizing of relationships greatly disturbed some staff. We were foregrounding the professional and formal dimension of the relationships. It was a significant change in "the way things were done". I had a premonition that sooner or later, what took place at such meetings would be disputed and agreements made/commitments given would be betrayed and I anticipated that I would have to draw on such accounts in another forum. I had a very strong sense of this.

I arranged to meet one particular teacher about whom there had been ongoing complaints. At our meeting, all the issues that we returned to repeatedly over the next years were raised. Thereafter, we had to intervene on numerous occasions in the teacher's classes. We met with the teacher and successive union representatives to attempt to resolve the issues, but to no avail. We made strenuous efforts to remove any obstacles that the teacher claimed hindered their management of their classes – increasing resources, employing an extra teacher in that subject to reduce the numbers in the classes, providing extra training for the teacher – but the only effect of all of this was to increase the teacher's distrust of me and of the deputy principal.

This continued for a number of years. One day at the beginning of term, a serious incident occurred involving this teacher. After an interaction with me around the teacher's responsibilities, the teacher completely lost it in the staff room. Eye witness reports said that the person went mad, kicking over furniture and in the process injuring another member of staff who arrived down to my office distraught. This member of staff reported that the teacher's eyes had been dancing in their head and that the person had been frothing and foaming at the mouth and had shouted that the Deputy Principal and I had been choreographing evil against the teacher concerned for the previous four years. The teacher left the staff room and the following day called in sick.

To state the obvious, I could not have predicted what happened. I have had, on numerous occasions, fantasies that a member of staff would attack me in the course of a difficult conversation, but this was the first time someone actually became violent. The staff were very shocked. I had never dealt with anything as explosive as this and never imagined that I would have to do so. Some staff immediately began to blame me for having "brought this on" and among themselves were saying that I had conducted a concerted campaign against this teacher. I made a brief statement to all the staff immediately after the teacher had left the premises giving the "facts" of what had taken place and refuting the teacher's allegations. Then, I did nothing else, but waited to see what would happen.

Six months later, the secretary got a phone call from the teacher to say that the person intended to return to school the following week. I asked to meet the teacher prior to their return, but this request was refused. I then got a phone call from the teachers' union to say that if I attempted to stop the teacher's return, they would initiate formal proceedings. I got legal advice and went to the Board of Management with the advice. The Board requested that a psychiatric assessment be sought for the teacher confirming that the person was fit to return to work. Eventually after months of wrangling, the assessment took place. It found the person unfit and a risk to the safety of all concerned. After a defined period of a year's sick leave, the teacher's salary was stopped. Several other assessments were conducted by us all leading to the same opinion. The teacher obtained other assessments certifying that the teacher was perfectly fit to return and that any problems were caused by the ongoing bullying of the principal. Eventually the teachers' union decided to bring me and the school to a labor court to seek payment of wages and reinstatement of the teacher in their position. Such hearings are open to the public and depending on the case the national newspapers will have someone in attendance.

The day before the hearing the teacher wrote to the head of the order who are the Trustees of the school saying that the case was likely to be in the papers and that there was potential for huge damage to the school. It was not too late for the trustees to reinstate the teacher and put a stop to my behavior. So, I got an alarmed phone call from one of the trustees to know if I could not sort this out at the eleventh hour and avoid any coverage in the papers. I said I couldn't – wouldn't.

We were met by a number of journalists when we walked in. We only found out who the judge was when we arrived. Our legal team informed us that he had a reputation for being very unpredictable. This was born out within the morning. He ruled that although the matter at issue was strictly a payment of wages claim, all information would be allowable including the teacher's allegations of bullying. There was enormous potential for a circus in the full glare of the media who were gathered to see a prestigious school on the mat. I asked our legal team to request a short adjournment and directed them to withdraw from the tribunal. I was determined that I was going to retain as much control as I could as to what conversations took place and to be vigilant about noticing the critical moments in negotiating control. Withdrawing from the tribunal was a statement about the parameters within which I would participate in a "conversation" with the court about the issues. I was going to contest this case on the playing field that I had chosen if at all possible.

We walked out. It was unprecedented. The chairman was apoplectic. For the next two days, the claimant's side presented their evidence and made disparaging and damning remarks about me, all of which were reported very negatively in the media, e.g. that I was lacking in compassion, was unchristian and was a bully. I found the exposure awful. I had to allay the anxiety of my family, of the Board, of the staff, and of the leadership team of the Order, never mind my own. I kept asking myself how things got to this point. Could I have sorted all of this out informally or just ignored the problems? Sure there is one – at least one – in every school. I remember sitting in a coffee shop reading a particularly vitriolic account about myself in one of the newspapers and wanting to get physically sick. Yet to do other than what I was doing did not feel like an option. It seemed to me that there would be no point in doing the job unless I went down this route. Of that I was absolutely convinced and full of doubt. While my conviction wavered in the face of the media coverage and everyone else's anxiety, there was never any question of giving in to it. I was hyper anxious and stoical.

The judge decided to exercise his right to subpoena me to attend with all the files on this teacher and at a later date to answer questions. The files were enormous and very detailed which took the judge and the claimant's side by surprise. There was a detailed account of every incident and conversation involving this teacher.

As I had no option but to attend, we decided to re-enter the tribunal as full participants. We made this judgment because we felt that the negative publicity, which we had previously decided to take on the chin, was having a weakening effect on the resolve of the Board of Management and the Trustees, and unsettling the staff. The subpoena led us to think about how we could use our re-entry in our interests even to the point of reversing our original position and contesting all of the allegations of bullying, if necessary, in the full glare of the media. At the same time, we still intended to avoid this if at all possible.

Had my intention changed? No, but I had to adapt to the changing circumstances, while remaining faithful to my initial intention. I presented our files and a summary of our position. We decided to make no reference to the bullying allegations. In preparation, the barrister ran through some of the questions I might be asked and suggested I read through all the files. I began to do so, and then gave up: it felt like cramming. My sense was that I was going to be thrown back on myself. The only advice I got from my legal people was to avoid trying to be the perfect witness. I should try "to come across as genuine". If I did not know something I should say so. An occasional mistake would not go amiss. I was told that I could not control what questions were asked, how people reacted to my answers or how the media reported what I said. I told myself that I could control how I related in the present moment to what was happening *as it was happening*. I put the files away and decided to rely on my lived-in knowledge of all that had taken place and my ability not to react to people, but to think on my feet. That is how I prepared for what might arise. It felt very simple to me. All I had to do was to tell the truth. I did not have to "act genuine". That was my intention.

As I began to give evidence, I can only describe the experience as akin to getting into a groove (Barrett, 1998). I was completely present to myself and to those surrounding me. I would describe it as a critical reflexive embodied consciousness. I got a feel for it straight away. I was in sync with myself, listening to the tone and volume of my voice, watching my eye contact, my use of my hands, the tilt of my head while focusing completely on what I was saying. I maintained eye contact with the chairman at all times. I did not advert to my non-verbal actions: it just all came together and I did not have to think about any of it. I relaxed into it; *something came over me and I felt controlled and in control*. Paradoxically, in not trying to exert any control or follow a pre-prepared script, I felt in control from the first minute. I had been composed and was composing myself. I was acting genuine and being genuine in acting/genuinely acting. I did not plan to perform like this. It happened quite naturally and spontaneously. This was intentionally manipulative and authentically me. The reader may find this statement provocative. I do not intend it to be so. I was not "acting" manipulatively. I was intentionally influencing proceedings while being truthful. Immediately, I began giving my evidence, my intention developed into completely neutralizing what I took to be the acidic environment I had entered. I had this intention, in germ, before I began, but it took shape and developed as soon as I began to speak.

The cross-examination by the teacher's barrister lasted the whole of the next day. There was a stark sense of being on my own and of having to rely on my ability to improvise. You can only improvise if you are immersed in your craft, whatever that may be, and have rehearsed your performance at length. I did so against a background of painstaking preparation, in-depth knowledge, and lengthy experience of having thought on my feet and also knowing that I could have confidence that I would not be provoked. I went in fully equipped to deal with whatever came up: I was not like the proverbial emperor without any clothes. While I did not have a whole series of moves prepared – I had worked out certain responses to possibly awkward questions if they were asked – I had a clear sense of intention going in to present myself as the honest broker in the situation, even the victim of circumstances and to confine the conversation to the issues that I considered to be relevant to the court and not be drawn into responding to accusations of bullying. Above all, I did not want to be experienced in a way that only confirmed the accusations of the claimant's barrister that I was a bully. This was the hardest part to get right. How did I go about it? I tried in preparing for the case and in the box to imaginatively access what a range of others listening to me might be thinking of me, as well as how I would desire them to see me and to keep relating to that as I was speaking. A consultant, whose help I sought, pointed out how quickly I go on the defensive if I take up another's comments as indicating a negative attitude toward me. I then sound exactly as I imagine the other sees me! I had to take up the attitude of the others, as Mead (1934) would put it, and in doing so to respond to that take as I desired to be taken up. I had to imagine myself as having the resources to do so. I also had information that the chairman was very keen to row back from the oppositional stance he had taken and the provocative comments he had made. So, I was improvising *and* I was following a very definite strategy based on preparation, information and training. I was well prepared to wing it.

I was particularly receptive in the moment to the cues the barrister gave me to connect with her story and develop it in a way that served my purposes. I joined with her and transformed the conversation from within to suit my purposes. It strikes me how closely connected control is to being able to be receptive to what is happening within the interaction at any moment. I was receptive to what emerged, but I maintain that I was prepared for most of what emerged. While the barrister's questions or strategies could not have been predicted beforehand, I was neither surprised nor thrown by anything that emerged. For example, when she criticized the lack of human resource personnel, I agreed with her and then told the tribunal what my qualifications were. She accused me of not protecting this teacher. In response, I referred to the teacher by their first name, expressed my genuine sympathy and broadened out my duty of care to foreground the protection of the children while also acknowledging my responsibility to protect the adults including this teacher. I contended that my actions were ultimately compassionate even to this teacher. She made several attempts to show that I had failed in my duty to investigate the incident in the staff room. I responded that to do so would have been a breach of natural justice to the teacher as the person was on sick leave. I also said that such an investigation would have forced teachers to take sides and that I wasn't willing to put the responsibility for dealing with the situation on anyone but myself. I was the manager. I used her accusation as a cue to go back over the incident and portray in detail and in as unemotive a manner as possible, what took place. I used vivid language, for example, saying that the teacher had "gone mad", to convey a heightened sense of the situation and to paint what I thought was an accurate picture for the tribunal and the media. I was being provocative in order to provoke understanding into how sudden and shocking the incident had been in the moment, not in order to provoke a reaction for its own sake. Throughout all of this, I kept drawing on what I thought the chairman and the journalists thought of me.

The phrase "painting pictures" came to mind as soon as she began to cross-examine me. The facts had to be told in a persuasive narrative. I was not spinning a story or making something up, I was depicting as vividly as I could my experience of what took place in order that I could offer the best possible account in the circumstances. I felt convinced that this was the right thing to do. The more she criticized my handling of the incident, the more I dwelt on what happened in detail and kept repeating the same words in different combinations, especially the phrase "gone mad", I was completely present within the conversation, aware of how I was coming across as I was responding to her. I was most conscious of this in my use of my voice. I kept monitoring whether or not there was any edge coming into it. I said that I had no option, but to take the action I took. I was caught in the middle of events not of my making. I had to convey a sense of being the one put upon without appearing to be manipulating anyone to feel sorry for me. At one and the same time, I was truthful and strategic, ethically manipulative. I was responding to the audiences as I thought they saw me with a view to transforming their perception of how I wanted them to see me, i.e. as in control and reasonable, fair and compassionate, in contrast to how I imagined they might be at risk of seeing me.

The media coverage the following morning was very negative about the other side's case, devastating in fact. All the papers carried headlines and photographs of the teacher. I felt very sorry for the teacher. While I had no control over what they had written about me some months ago or about what they wrote now about me or about the teacher, I had an opportunity to influence them by offering the best possible account I could give and I did so. I did so in what I adjudged to be the best interests of the school.

Several months later, the teacher agreed to resign their position and take early retirement. We were informed that counsel advised the union and the teacher that there was little possibility of reinstatement or of significant damages.

The struggle for self-mastery

I want to "write in" what, on reading, may seem absent to the reader, that is, the experience of inner struggle to master myself, so as to be able to be present to all that emerged and influence, if not control, what happened. This narrative has the most possibility of being a liberating one if it is created on an ongoing basis with another or others capable of being "ruthlessly compassionate" (Senge *et al.*, 2005) with me. Taylor makes the point that the social nature of our identity entails our dependency of our self-interpretation on intersubjective networks, "a web of interlocution" as he refers to it (1989). If I write only that I myself may have something to read and speak only to hear myself talk, then a narcissistic self-regard, devoid of reflexivity, is the likely outcome. The web of interlocution I have found most useful is that of supervision. I talk with and listen to someone else in supervision because I trust neither the ferocity of my ruthlessness nor the possibly collusive nature of my compassion. It has enabled me to include all of the thoughts and feelings that are triggered in me in response to work as I narrate and re-narrate my experience as principal. It affords me the mental space to tell of my experience and to remain detached and involved. It enables me to "retrieve" and fortify a sense of conviction that feels very fragile and strong at the same time. It offers an opportunity to explore the roots of that conviction and to evaluate what of it is appropriately zealous and what in it risks becoming fanatical and obsessive. It enables me to contain my anxiety about the task and to look at the judgments I am making that are engendered by my perception of their anti-task behavior. It provides an opportunity for the shadow side of my desire for power to emerge (Guggenbuhl-Craig, 1971), in particular, the desire to crush, to seek revenge, to intimidate, to provoke, to put it up to people, and the associated feelings of frustration, anger, venom and omnipotence. In short, it enables me to develop a rigorous reflexivity in regard to my responses and to be accountable.

Finally, all of that self-examination in the presence of another enables me to distil out what belongs only to this situation in work and to return to the school with only that distillation. The rest I leave behind. This to me is what *has* to take place in order to have a detached involvement and to exercise self-control. It involves a self-emptying, a purging of my desires, a dying to self that I have found intensely painful. The most painful part is being revealed to myself, having the shadow brought to light. I know my capacity to be ruthless, to be violent and my desire to act on this. I will return to this process of self-emptying later when dealing with Senge's work.

In order to manage, I had to manage myself. I could not be under the control of that shadow when I was being cross-examined or at any stage when I was interacting with the staff. This self-examination gave me a sense of certainty, because I felt that I had dredged out everything in my attitude that belonged only to me. I know how hard won and momentary my self-mastery is and thus how fragile it seems. It does not feel arrogant: I was and am hyper aware of my desire to act with ruthless abandon and the fragility of the control I have over that desire in this moment. In distilling out of that desire what was only connected to the task in hand, I felt reconnected to the task and to why I was doing what I was doing at the level of my deepest convictions. Every time I feel that desire to crush others, I have to re-enter that space and re-evaluate my desires. The control has to be achieved moment to moment, but my experience is that *I have achieved that moment to moment*. I suspect that level of self-control enrages some of the staff and may have contributed to the particular member of staff at the center of the narrative losing it. I own that this self-control can drive people berserk.

Where I recognize this level of self-control, is actually when I feel relaxed and almost outside myself while feeling completely attentive and involved in what is at hand. That was what the experience of the tribunal was like: an experience of presence to myself, of detached involvement. The presence was achievement. It was also an absence, of everything in me that did not belong to what was at hand and that was not in accord with my deepest desires and convictions. The paradox is that I felt most myself in having let go of those desires. I felt that I conveyed a ruthless compassion that felt ethical and authentic (Taylor, 1991). I was not acting. I was not improvising. I knew myself, I was completely present, critically reflexively conscious of myself and I felt able to handle whatever arose, completely in control and trusting that the conversation would evolve in the best interests of all.

In a previous draft of this chapter, I omitted including any mention of the struggle involved in achieving such mastery, albeit momentary. Why? I was afraid that disclosing it would dilute the achievement. I was also afraid that you the reader and others yet to read this would attend to my descriptions of my shadow side as I have referred to it, and not to how I had overcome it in this situation. I struggle to find a language for including vulnerability and fragility in a way that enhances my description of how I manage. I think my speaking and writing would be provocative in the sense of invoking curiosity rather than evoking a reaction if I could learn to offer more nuanced descriptions of what I do and why I do it. I have been told repeatedly by superiors and supervisors that I don't reveal any of the process of agonizing/struggling that I actually experience in my speaking and in my non-verbal actions. I revealed none of it in the first draft of this chapter though I lived through the most isolating and self-doubting time of my life. It felt that revealing this would betray my having mastered and harnessed my drives, contained my anxiety and braved my fears. Instead the effect of not doing so was to impoverish the richness of the description of the process of mastering myself. It was also intensely provocative to a group of readers of the initial draft of the chapter, a study group for the Doctor of Management program. Their reaction mirrored the response of the Trustees and of the staff to me over the last number of years. The intention that the narrative would be primarily about my struggle for self-mastery was lost to those reading it. The reader cannot read what is not written. The struggle was written *out* of the narrative and some of what might have been most provocative was lost. A reader may be led to amplify the apparent ruthlessness in the absence of any evidence of such a struggle on my part to be ruthlessly compassionate.

Self-mastery in the work of Peter Senge

The themes of mastery, discipline and presence are taken up by Peter Senge and his colleagues in the Society for Organisational Learning. I intend to draw on *The Fifth Discipline* (1994) and *Presence* (2005) to examine what insights Senge's account yields in the light of my experience and where it falls short.

Senge (1994: 141) describes what he means by personal mastery and how it can be fostered in the learning organization. It embodies two underlying movements:

1   Continually clarifying what is important to us;
2   Learning to see current reality more clearly.

The ability to focus on ultimate intrinsic desires, not just on secondary goals, is key to personal mastery (ibid.: 148). Why do we want it? Senge claims that "we want personal mastery because we want it" (ibid.: 144). Connecting to one's ultimate intrinsic desires is to live consistently with one's purpose (ibid.: 148). Personal mastery must be a discipline. Why? It is a process of continually focusing and refocusing on what one truly wants, on one's visions (ibid.: 149). The courage to take a stand for one's vision distinguishes people of personal mastery (ibid.: 150). The mastery is evident in one's ability to creatively hold in tension one's vision and the present reality seen accurately. He then mentions several quasi-virtues of such an individual: able to integrate reason and intuition, connected to the world, compassionate and committed to the whole (ibid.: 167). In order to achieve this, one has to balance "inquiry into and advocacy of one's position" (ibid.: 202). One must be conscious of the gap between one's professed theories, what Argyris (1991) called "espoused theory" and one's "theory-in-use". To do this one may need a "ruthlessly compassionate partner". Later, he talks about the need for "reflective openness" that leads people to look inward (Senge, 1994: 277). This openness is a change in spirit and it facilitates dialogue. Dialogue requires the development of skills, but it also requires a "fundamental spiritual disposition" (ibid.: 285).

When I read this initially, I felt myself resonating with him and yet something felt missing. I kept writing in the margins: *how* am I to achieve this mastery? He talks about self-mastery as a process, but *never gives the reader the process*. It was in reading Senge that it was brought home to me that I wasn't doing so either. Senge doesn't give an account of what needs to happen for self-mastery to happen. He asserts that both skills and a fundamental disposition are needed to develop openness. To what skills is he referring? How would I develop this disposition? Is there another book I have to read? It has all the marks of a seductive self-help manual for the aspiring manager that promises that if you read it, you will achieve mastery. What it leaves out is a detailed account of how one is to get there. It fails to acknowledge what I mentioned earlier as critical: such mastery of self involves pain and struggle that demand a self-emptying and a death. Urging us to commit ourselves to the quest for our personal mastery and to be a model for others makes it seem as though all we have to do is akin to making a New Year's resolution and it will fall into place. I also left out an account of my struggle in an earlier draft. What is it that led me and leads him to do so? How is this related to the audiences to whom I imagine I am speaking?

I am also left asking why would I want to put myself through the pain of mastering myself? This comes back to my fundamental sense of conviction or calling (Senge, 1994: 144). Wherefore this conviction? How might that be evoked in someone? To say that we want it because we want it is not self-evident to me. To appeal to some woolly desire to model mastery to all and sundry is insufficient. The importing of religious language into a secular context without rigorously grounding such language in the everyday work experience of managers is not credible and the feeling I have is that it is being used as a way of heading off criticism by appealing to a transcendent and deeply subjective experience. How are you supposed to evaluate the difference between a self-mastering manager and a deeply convinced fanatic?

There is no structure offered for evaluating the effectiveness of any of this except the testimony of chosen managers. Similarly, his valuing of dialogue offers little in the way of direction as to what conversational structures or modes of facilitating such conversations by these self-mastered managers would look like and how one would create a context where people would be willing to consider the possibility that it might be worth aspiring to a reflective openness (ibid.: 277–81). The difficulty in all of this is that I cannot disagree with dialogue or any of the other laudable ideas and motifs presented by Senge, but they do not offer any detailed rigorous account of the process of achieving dialogue.

I also take issue with his contention that people with a high level of personal mastery are always learning, they never "arrive" (ibid.: 142). You do not possess it, it is a process. There is, in my opinion, an abundance of such faux humility in the literature of self-development and leadership. To contend otherwise is not arrogant, but actually is an effort to be more accountable. I contended that in that tribunal, I *arrived*. Yes, if I had to deal with another fraught situation again, I would have to do an immense amount of preparation and reflection, but I would do it with the confidence that I had arrived before and I could do so again. This, albeit temporary, localized certainty is written out of Senge and denied by postmodern thinking as being possible to attain. The certainty of which I speak is not founded in arrogance, but in a rigorous examination of my motivating values as evidenced in my actions. The lack of such rigor in this description of self-mastery is what risks arrogance. Adverting briefly to the process nature of self-mastery is no substitute for accounting for how such arrogance is to be avoided.

While availing of the phrase "ruthless compassion" repeatedly, they do not explore the "ruthless" part of this and fail to mention it in the list of qualities of the self-mastering individual. Something crucial is lost in my experience if the paradox in this phrase is dissolved. The ruthlessness connects to a basic drive and a sense of potency that has been integral to my energy in leadership. My sense is of the absence of conflict in Senge's descriptions of relationships involving those on the way to self-mastery and in his giving pride of place to dialogue where we suspend assumptions, position each other as colleagues and develop this reflective openness. My suspicion is that "dialogue" is often proposed as a morally preferable way of relating that can potentially do violence to people by papering over and not engaging with the real, significant and ongoing differences between parties, an engagement that will necessitate conflict. I chose to compose a narrative based on events that highlighted my acting ruthlessly and compassionately. I managed to do so because I had set aside all of the ruthlessness and compassion that did not belong to this situation and avoided splitting off ruthlessness from compassion.

Finally, Senge's self-mastery is of the individual self as is my description of my struggle to do so. One piece of work I want to do is to examine how such self-mastery and control might be understood if I were to think about the individual as social, drawing on the work of Mead (1934), Dewey (1934) and others.

The book *Presence* was written by Senge in collaboration with a number of colleagues. It is an attempt to situate self-mastery in a spiritual and ecological framework and to inquire into how change referred to as a "shift" actually takes place. They are interested in inquiring into this shift as a collective phenomenon and into how a collective capacity for this shift could be cultivated (Senge *et al.*, 2004: 12). They maintain that most change processes are superficial because they don't generate the depth of understanding and commitment required for sustaining change in demanding circumstances (ibid.: 87). This accords with my experience of participating in many such "processes" in religious life. They are concerned with the deeper dimension of transformational change (ibid.: 15). They devise a threefold "U process" comprising:

1   Sensing, immersing oneself in the reality of the situation;
2   Presencing, perception arising from the highest possibility that connects self and whole;
3   Realizing, acting in a natural flow where one is simultaneously engaged and detached (ibid.: 86).

They maintain that the basic difference between this and the way change is usually understood is that the self, the group and the world "are inescapably connected" (ibid.: 92). The self is not reacting to a world outside or creating something new apart from others or the world. Rather, "like the seed of a tree, it becomes the gateway for the coming into being of a new world". The experience is one of "unbroken awareness and action". As I understand it, the critical moment is at the bottom of this U when one moves into presencing. It involves letting go of our need to control, opening the way for a larger awareness and a sense of what is emerging. It is described as a decentering and expansion of the self. They acknowledge that "people often have great difficulty describing the experience" (ibid.: 102). Later they say that the only way to evoke a sense of the theory is through personal experience (ibid.: 206). Despite several readings and a background in a religious tradition, I had great difficulty in understanding what they were saying in regard to presencing. As the grip of what Varela refers to as the "localized self" diminishes – which I take to mean my habitual understanding of myself as a contained, boundaried individual – one's attention changes from "looking for" to "letting come" (ibid.: 103). Surrendering control evolves into surrendering commitment and committing oneself to a larger whole. One feels unable not to commit oneself: one feels compelled to commitment.

The relationship between self and the world is transformed. We move from seeing the world out there as it is, to seeing from inside the living processes underlying reality, to experiencing the world coming into being through us. Our will is transformed in seeing from within the forces that shape our reality and our part in how these forces might evolve. This crystallizes into a larger intention and an expanded self. They claim that what distinguishes the most successful leaders – what Senge in *The Fifth Discipline* would have termed those with personal mastery – is "their capacity to tap into and focus a larger intention". The source of their intention is larger: "action arises as a sponta-neous product of the whole" (ibid.: 141). You do what obviously needs to be done. They seem to move from the individual self to the Self writ large, a global expanded self in which we are transformed and fulfilled by being part of a larger whole.

What do I make of this in the light of my experience of mastering myself? Once again, I find that I agree with the process they outline, in so far as I could get a grip of what they meant. That is one of the difficulties. If you have not had an experience similar to one of theirs, it is hard to pin down what they mean. The language drawn from a variety of religious traditions is meant to shed light on faith or spiritual experiences and may make sense to one who has had such experiences, but to a manager unfamiliar with this and immersed in dealing with the everyday and urgent demands of his/her organization...? The effect on this reader was to leave me feeling somewhat excluded and at sea. As they suggest, I try to see things as they are, and talking through my views with supervisors and colleagues I am convinced that no significant change can happen until I and others "decenter" ourselves, i.e. manage to empty ourselves of all that will get in the way of the "primary task" of the organization (Obholzer and Zagier Roberts, 1994). That may lead to my committing myself to something more/larger than my personal project or intention. The kernel of the process – the bottom of the U, as they refer to it – involves a shift in understanding which is described as a "mystery": "This inversion of the relational web of self and world cannot be reduced to words, and people experience it in different ways"(ibid.: 103). As an explication of the nature of change, I am left none the wiser: the nature of the shift is a mystery. I found this very frustrating and it makes it very difficult to critique what they are saying. If you haven't had an analogous experience, where are you left with this? No detailed account is given of the how – i.e. the process – of the shift.

As in *The Fifth Discipline*, little explanation is actually given as to how "the process of cultivation" of change is to take place. Griffin makes precisely this point in reference to the earlier work when he identifies the problem as one of defining the process by which he/she becomes aware of the need to change pref-erences (2002: 47). They extol the value of meditation on numerous occasions and in order to assist groups make the shift, they suggest facilitation. How does meditation work to create the conditions for such a shift and is this to be norm-ative for all managers? What kind of facilitation do they have in mind? It is as though this should be self-evident to the reader. The outline of the threefold U process conveys a sense of an ordered sequential movement to realization. Time is linear. I notice in the narrative that I describe intention in a similar way, i.e. there is a before and an after. Yet my experience of such a process fits more with Griffin's notion of time as "circular in the sense that the emerging future is constructed, as is the understanding of the past, in the self-organizing processes of interaction in the living present" (ibid.: 15). I go back and forward in the present in what feels like a much messier process. I do and I don't shift in that orderly progressive U movement. However, I do think there is an attempt in *Presence* to address the nature of changing that is absent in most of the literature and an effort is made to include a spiritual dimension, albeit in a way that seems subjective, self-justifying and closed to criticism.

Griffin (2002) criticizes Senge in *The Fifth Discipline* for the both/and theory of leaders and of leadership in organizations. The idea of self-mastery is located in the autonomous individual and the idea of leadership emerges in the systemic self-organization of the whole with the notions of dialogue (as developing a pool of common meaning), teams and shared vision describing how we participate in this whole. Griffin's point is that, in this theory, the leader stands outside the system and alone exercises freedom fully. Everyone else's ethical choices are reduced "to a constant search for a freely chosen submission to a transcendent whole" (ibid.: 48). Senge's positing of a transcendental whole, i.e. a metaphysical basis, for his theory of leadership, means that those participating "are not focused on the everyday potential emerging from conflict and difference" (ibid.: 79). Griffin perhaps does not allow for the possibility that one might freely choose to submit to authority and to a transcendent reality in a way that enhances one's sense of autonomy while *at the same time*, constantly renegotiating what that means for one to do so. To live it fully, one cannot disown either part of the equation. The possible loss of autonomy in Senge's model of which Griffin warns, seems reasonable, but seems particularly postmodern and seems to have in mind a particular notion of autonomy that rightly needs to be protected. The basic assumption is that it is not tenable to imagine a greater freedom and an enlarged sense of self arising from letting go of the self, as Senge puts it, and letting come what one is now open to once one's self is no longer in the way.

Joas makes a similar point to Griffin in his critique of Taylor. He states that we have lost a metaphysical grounding of the good and thus what is valuable in itself is only accessible to us from the perspective of our actions (Joas, 2000: 143). It is assumed that "metaphysics" is for a bygone age. No attempt is made to retrieve a metaphysical framework from within our experience. There is a need to critically examine the pragmatic assumptions informing both Griffin's and Joas' evaluation of the positions articulated by Senge and others. What has been lost is the paradoxical relationship between freedom and obedience, autonomy and submission, metaphysics and the everyday.

I do not think Senge gets it right, but he asks the question and struggles to find a language to honor this paradox. In my opinion, this work has not been done in organizational literature. The kernel of this paradox is expressed succinctly in a piece from Martin Buber that Senge uses:

> The free man is he who wills without arbitrary self-will.... He must sacrifice his puny, unfree will, which is controlled by things and instincts, to his grand will.... Then he intervenes no more, but at the same time, he does not let things merely happen. He listens to what is emerging from himself, to the course of being in the world; not in order to be supported by it, but in order to bring it to reality as it desires.
>
> (Senge, 1994: 147–8)

Arriving is managing to hold that paradox. My experience of myself in my way of dealing with this teacher was of having to sacrifice my puny unfree will. In the course of doing so, something came over me and I felt led to respond to what emerged while feeling in control. The experience was of emergent control.

What Griffin criticizes in Senge is, in my words, the "outsourcing" of the basis of leadership and ethics in organizations, whether the sources be higher wholes or transcendent realities, etc. For him the ethical interpretation of any action is to be found *in the action itself* (2002: 19). The meanings and significance of actions cannot be known in advance: what is valuable is only accessible from the perspective of our actions, "the actions in which it is constituted and operative for us" (Joas, 2000: 143). This is the consequence of a pragmatic starting point: the experience of value is located in action. As I indicated earlier in speaking of intention, my experience is of uncovering my deepest intentions in action, recognizing them through interacting with significant interlocutors such that I can say that I have discovered them in action and interaction, but my experience of this discovery is of it being akin to a *recovery* and recognition of that with which I feel most at home, that accords with my deepest sense of self. This sense of conviction feels as though it has always been there waiting to be discovered. I know it when I discover it. I feel that my struggle to master myself is an expression of a quest that *draws* me to retrieve that which is of most value to me and that which enables me to transcend myself.

Charles Taylor takes up these ideas in his work *Sources of the Self*. His purpose is to locate "moral sources outside the self" not through a metaphysical theory along the lines of the Platonists where the good was understood to be something independent of the person, but "through languages which resonate *within* him or her, the grasping of an order which is inseparably indexed to a personal vision" (Taylor, 1989: 510). Who we are is inseparable from how we interpret ourselves. Taylor examines how we do so in order to retrieve from within this interpreting our sources of value. Our self-understanding essentially involves our distinguishing between what we see to be of more and of less value. He distinguishes between weak and strong evaluations, the former being evaluations of whether or not a particular desire is practically realizable, the latter according to whether or not such a desire is desirable according to standards that feel as though they have been "given to us". He claims that in attempting to make the best possible sense of our lives, we arrive at what is for us at this moment the best possible articulation of our experience, the best possible account. It becomes self-evident that certain values are indispensable to us and not to act in accordance with these values is not an option. In this interpreting of our experience, we discover that what we value has a quality that feels independent of us. *We are convinced by these values.*

Stacey takes up the ideas of Joas, Dewey and Mead in holding that values are continually "arising" in social interaction. It follows that values are contingent upon the specific action situation in which we find ourselves. Dewey, he explains, held that such communicative interaction opens up human beings to each other, making possible the experience of self-transcendence, in which values arise in which there is a decentering of the self toward the other. How does this experience of interaction give rise to these values? What is the *source* of the values? It doesn't follow to me that they are contingent on the particular action situation. This sounds like a circular argument. Communicative interaction is as likely, and in my opinion more likely in itself, to lead to humans closing off than opening up to each other. What is it that creates the openness rather than closedness? Or is it something in particular ways of interacting rather than others? Is it something about the way the conversation/interaction is structured that creates the openness? Is it something that we cannot create of ourselves in our interaction, but can only wait to let come, as Senge puts it: a *being moved* to openness and out of closedness, which in the Christian tradition might be termed grace? Stacey also draws on Dewey's use of the imagination to explain how we feel compelled to act out of particular values. We idealize particular intense experiences as having a wholeness that is imaginary, but seems real because of the intensity of the experience and leads us to feel we have no alternative, but to act in a particular way. In this he differs from Taylor who, as I said above, holds that such values feel independent of us. Taylor while disavowing a return to a Platonic metaphysics of the good, intends to "retrieve buried goods" (Taylor, 1989: 520) and admits that he holds a theistic perspective, while not foregrounding it due to a lack of arguments (ibid.).

Ultimately, I was left disappointed that Taylor had not managed to hold the metaphysical and the pragmatic in tension together. It seems to me that he ultimately ends up in Platonic territory. I am dissatisfied with both Joas' and Taylor's description of the genesis of values. I am conscious of my own taken-for-granted assumptions that "my" values and intentions are individually mine and existed prior to the court case of which I have spoken. What would be the implications of really engaging with, for example, Mead's notion, that what I, the claimant, and the other parties in the court were doing was struggling to functionalize divergent cult values of which our differing intentions were a reflection? Such a perspective feels quite threatening, because I want/need to believe that there is a ground or source of value that is outside of the social. All of my life, I have been "given" to believe that there is. The nature and source of this givenness and my need for it and belief in it is material for much future reflection. Joas also can be criticized methodologically in a similar vein. While holding that values and norms must arise in an ethics based on the perspective of the actor (Joas, 2000: 182), Joas never actually delves into the perspective of any actor in any contingent situation to tease out his views. His writing retreats again and again into a discussion of ideas while purporting to combine a theory of the contingent genesis of values and a conception of moral universalism (ibid.: 169).

Conclusion

In conclusion, I hope that this chapter has provoked you the reader to inquire into your notions of intention, value, purpose and the genesis of these. What is not clear to me is how to hold the metaphysical and the pragmatic together in a way that does justice to what-is-good-in-itself-for-us and what is good-in-itself. I am reluctant to disown the realm of metaphysics for the lure of pragmatism, but at this time I am not sure how to describe the relationship between the two in a way that does justice to my experience of feeling called by something that seems "outside" of me, yet is something that I continually find within my practice in work. I suggest that narratives of our practice offer a way into exploring such apparently contradictory positions. The story I have told has arisen out of my involvement in managing on a day-to-day basis where I have determined to constructively engage staff around the task of the school over a lengthy period of time as a means of carrying out the task and negotiating what that task is at one and the same time. Doing so has inevitably led to conflict and I would contend that the negotiation of what values mean in practice occurs through conflict. Challenging the way things are done as I have is a risky venture.

To act in this way may involve one being ruthlessly compassionate. I have come across very little written about the experience of managers being ruthlessly compassionate. It requires a mastery of self, a concept espoused by Senge among others, but Senge omits the experience of struggle and the asceticism it requires. I find the struggle everyday to master myself extremely painful, demanding a kind of asceticism that I describe as a rigorous reflexivity. The process of doing so is omitted by most accounts of managing change. In so doing, they do no justice to the demand to engage oneself that is a precondition if one is to constructively engage others over a lengthy period of time and avoid the accusations that one is merely a bully or a zealot instead of truly taking care of the relationships by being mindful of the task.

References

Abbey, R. (ed.) (2004) *Charles Taylor*, Cambridge: Cambridge University Press.
Argyris, C. (1991) "Teaching smart people how to learn", *Harvard Business Review* 69, 3: 99–109.
Barrett, F. J. (1998) "Creativity and improvisation in jazz and organizations: Implications for organizational learning", *Organizational Science*, 9, 5: 605–22.
Baur, S. (1997) *The Intimate Hour: Love and Sex in Psychotherapy*, Boston: Houghton Mifflin Company.
Buber, M. (1961) *Between Man and Ma*, London: Fontana Collins.
Buber, M. (1970) *I and Thou*, Edinburgh: T&T Clark.
Carotenuto, A. (1996) *To Love To Betray*, Wilmette: Chiron Publications.

Carotenuto, A. (1989) *Eros and Pathos: Shades of Love and Suffering*, Toronto: Inner City Publications.

Dewey, J. (1934) *A Common Faith*, New Haven: Yale University Press.

Gergen, K. J. (1991) *The Saturated Self: Dilemmas of Identity in Contemporary Life*, New York: Basic Books.

Griffin, D. (2002) *The Emergence of Leadership: Linking Self-Organization and Ethics*, London: Routledge.

Guggenbuhl-Craig, A. (1971) *Power in the Helping Professions*, Dallas: Spring Publications.

Hirschhorn, L. (1997) *Reworking Authority: Leading and Following in the Postmodern Organization*, Cambridge: MIT.

Joas, H. (2000) *The Genesis of Values*, Cambridge: Polity Press.

Mead, G. H. (1934) *Mind, Self & Society*, Chicago: University of Chicago Press.

MacIntyre, A. (1981) *After Virtue*, London: Duckworth.

Murdoch, I. (1970) *The Sovereignty of Good*, Routledge: London.

Obholzer, A. and Zagier Roberts, V. (eds.) (1994) *The Unconscious at Work: Individual and Organizational Stress in the Human Service*, London: Routledge.

Oliver, C (2002) "Critical-appreciative inquiry: Reworking a consultancy discourse", in Peck, E. (ed.) *An Introduction to Organisational Development in the NHS*, London: Radcliffe Medical Press.

Oliver, C. and Brittain, G. (2001) "Systemic constructionist management: A study of the discursive moral features of an episode of management education", talk given at Conference on *Organizational Discourse: Word-views, Work-views and World-views*, King's College, London.

Rorty, R. (1989) *Contingency, Irony, Solidarity*, Cambridge: Cambridge University Press.

Senge, P. (1994) *The Fifth Discipline: The Art and Practice of the Learning Organization*, New York: Doubleday.

Senge, P., Scharmer, C. O., Jaworski, J. and Flowers, B. S. (2004) *Presence: Human Purpose and the Field of the Future*, Cambridge: SoL.

Shaw, P. (2002) *Changing Conversations in Organizations: A Complexity Approach to Change*, London: Routledge.

Shotter, J. (1993) *Conversational Realities: Constructing Life through Language*, London: Sage.

Stacey, R. "Complexity at the 'edge' of the basic-assumption group", in Gould, L. and Stapley, L. F. (2001) *Psychodynamics of Organizations*, New York: Karnac.

Stacey, R. D., Griffin, D. and Shaw, P. (2000) *Complexity and Management: Fad or Radical Challenge to Systems Thinking?*, London: Routledge.

Taylor, C. (1989) *Sources of the Self: The Making of the Modern Identity*, Cambridge: Cambridge University Press.

Taylor, C. (1991) *The Ethics of Authenticity*, Cambridge, MA: Harvard University Press

Taylor, C. (2002) *Varieties of Religion Today: William James Revisited*, Cambridge, MA: Harvard University Press.

Editors' introduction to Chapter 6

Stephen Billing, an independent consultant, describes his involvement in a change management project in a high technology company. The change in question is a move to a new head office building, which unfortunately turns out to be too small for the rapidly growing company. This problem is to be dealt with by assigning staff to different, newly created categories of employees, some of whom will have a fixed desk, others will have to use whatever desk they can find, while yet others will have to work from their cars and homes. This move to a new building, accompanied by changes in ways of working, is expected to raise resistance and so require some kind of change management. The author of this chapter approaches this situation with the view that change management here means providing people with opportunities to talk about and work through the issues raised for them by the proposed changes. However, his clients in the organization want to avoid conversation over which they might lose control and propose instead a high energy event which they hope will "convert" people to a favorable reception of the change. From Billing's perspective, the clients are looking for a propaganda event to give a favorable "spin" on the change and are looking for a consultant who will conduct the public relations exercise. However, this approach is not one that Billing feels at all comfortable with.

The central issue then has to do with conflicting views about how an effective change management project is to be conducted. Billing deals with the conflict by apparently agreeing to what the client wants but keeps open the option of influencing the project into another direction once it commences. As in previous chapters, conflict immediately gives rise to the various possibilities for compromise and as before this immediately raises issues of values and ethics. Is it ethical to continue working on a project one fundamentally disagrees with? Is it ethical to assuage one's unease about doing so by retaining an undisclosed intention to change the way of working as the project develops? These are the questions Billing deals with in this chapter. In the course of dealing with these questions he explores the relationship between the techniques of organizational development and propaganda. He points to how the fields of Organization Development and Public Relations actually have much in common and seem to be merging together. Billing reflects on his work as an attempt to make sense of this emerging ethical challenge.

6 The role of propaganda in managing organizational change

Ethics, conflict and compromise in consulting

Stephen Billing

In this chapter, I describe an organizational change project in which I was involved as a consultant. I explore the establishment of a relationship between client and consultant, the design of a change intervention and the facilitation of groups as key components of typical approaches to organizational change. What came out of this experience, for me, was a realization that as people attempt to influence the outcomes of organizational change in order to stay in control, they can easily become caught in collusive processes of manipulation, often without being aware of it. It becomes important, then, for people to acknowledge what they are doing.

The first section of this chapter posits that the process of engaging a change consultant is not merely establishing a contract and therefore separate from the consulting assignment itself, but that the interactions that occur during the contracting process affect the way the change processes themselves evolve. Inevitably ethical questions arise during the contracting process and this chapter argues that viewing ethics as arising in ongoing processes of negotiation is more closely related to experience than the dominant view of ethics in relation to Kant's universal standard. The next section briefly summarizes the literature in two disciplines: planned change interventions, and public relations, propaganda and publicity. There are some note-worthy similarities between these disciplines which, it is suggested, may signal the blurring of the boundaries between organization development and public relations. The final section explores facilitation of groups in organizational change, agreeing with Shaw (2002) that the widespread distinction between process and content has led facilitators to design the desired patterns of interaction in advance, even though these patterns of interaction are not under the control of any one individual. Process facilitation is then needed because unwanted patterns of conversation will continue to arise in spite of the best group process design.

Unacknowledged attempts to stay in control are at work at many levels in an organizational change program. The undiscussable nature of these attempts to stay in control reduces awareness that they exist, and this inevitably leads to collusion and manipulation amongst those involved. Surfacing these unacknowledged motives and making them discussable can help consultants, clients and managers be more effective in organizational change processes.

Preparing to move to a new site

My associate Richard and I put forward a joint consultancy proposal to Sinead, the HR project manager of TCorp, a technology corporation that has achieved great success in selling leading edge products to the youth market. The company has a very "funky" public image and a matching perception of their organization internally. Their advertising campaigns, aimed at young people, emphasize price, ease and "coolness", contributing to the huge popularity of their technology. The head office of the company was preparing to move into a brand new purpose-built building but their phenomenal growth rate meant that the building was already too small. They had, therefore, devised a way of accommodating increased numbers in the space through greater utilization of mobile technology, "hot desks" and shared spaces. Workspace was to be allocated according to work categories based on reliance on telephones and the degree of mobility required as follows: staff whose activities were mainly conducted over the telephone were configured into a call center; those whose activities required them to have a dedicated desk although they would not necessarily need the call center configuration; sales people whose jobs required them to be out of the office most of the time and so their cars would function as their offices; and those such as senior managers, who might be in and out of the office and so a "hot desk" would suit their needs. These different categories of workers immediately raise issues of status and identity, which I will refer to later on. Sinead wanted to find a provider to facilitate sessions for General Managers and people leaders, to help everyone prepare for moving into the new building and introduce the new identities and ways of working.

The client briefed us that:

> with the relocation rapidly approaching the time is right for General Managers and people leaders to translate the concepts and strategies into practical action so they can effectively manage the change in harmony with the relocation. They will need to address the practical implications of the move for their groups, make sense of the implications of the new ways of working for their teams, and plan how to manage the transition and bedding down over time of the new ways of working.

They wanted us to work with the internal project team and provider of public relations services. After Richard's initial conversations with the client, we proposed to undertake an initial assessment prior to designing and delivering a series of sessions for General Managers and middle managers. Our assessment proposed meeting with key parties including a sample of General Managers, people leaders and other staff, and reviewing organizational documentation. After this initial assessment, we proposed to design a workshop format in conjunction with the client, run the workshop as a pilot with a sample of key managers, and then amend and conduct the workshop for the rest of the people. With this approach we were confident we could design and facilitate the sessions required, and also undertake any other activities, trouble shooting and so on, that are often necessary in preparing for a move and new ways of operating.

From the proposals received, the client selected us as the provider, telling us that they had done so because they liked the approach we outlined and Richard's work for them in the past. However, they also told us that their budget was only half of what we had estimated our fee to be, and asked us whether, since they had largely designed the sessions already, we could simply facilitate the workshops without the initial assessment and proposed follow up work for the money they had available. Richard and I considered seriously whether to bow out at this stage due to not being able to run our full approach. We discussed at length the public relations company's ideas for the design of the sessions, which had been conceived as a highly structured, carefully programed event that would be fast-paced and high energy. For example, prior to a visit to the new site it was planned that the song "YMCA" would play at volume, and dancers wearing hard hats would come into the room of participants who would now be cast in the role of proposed visitors to the new site, receiving from the dancers hard hats and safety gear. Then they would carry out a safety briefing, after which the proposed visitors would have their palms scanned into a device to simulate security entry into the site. We concluded that what they were looking for was a master of ceremonies for the event, rather than a facilitator of the discussion and planning which we sensed would be needed. For example, the client had told Richard that the new ways of working meant re-allocation of laptops and fewer car spaces – there were issues of status and power associated with these two items which I saw as symptomatic of the portending changes to identity inherent in the new roles. I was also uncomfortable that the client had pleaded no budget for the facilitation of these events and yet seemed to be planning to spend big money on equipment and props.

Eventually, however, we decided that we would agree to the client's request, based on their assertion they had already undertaken a needs assessment and knew what was needed. The project was well down the track and they seemed quite desperate for our help as they were running out of time. I felt a strong desire to undertake the work as I had already spent considerable time and effort figuring out how we would approach the project, and I was reluctant to let go of it. I also had a gap in my calendar and the need to earn money. At the same time I felt some misgivings at the reduced scope of the work, the lack of time to prepare, and the reduced role Richard and I would play. Richard and I both disagreed with the highly programed nature of the events planned, but hoped we would be able to influence the client away from that design. At this point, I discovered that one of the key players in the project was Mary, a woman I had developed a good working relationship with on a previous project, and with whom I knew I would be able to speak frankly about the design of the session and the project in general, so this gave me a degree of confidence that we would be able to achieve a successful result.

The engagement process: contracts and ethics

The above ordered account sets out a clear sequence of events leading to a well-articulated consulting assignment. Richard and I have been invited to submit a proposal for a piece of work according to the terms of reference given to us by the client. They have expressed interest in hiring us but want to negotiate about the terms of reference, greatly reducing the scope of the work and altering its nature. This leaves me feeling uneasy because the client is proposing a very structured and planned series of sessions which do not seem to leave enough room for dealing with the messy and unexpected issues that my experience tells me are likely to arise. Nevertheless, we have decided to accept the offer to do a reduced and changed piece of work in the expectation that we can continue to negotiate its nature as we go through it. This is not a unique situation – I have faced it before and I expect many consultants and clients will have been in this situation before as well. The question is how one is to think about the relationship between consultant and client in such situations.

I discussed this situation with my learning group on the doctoral research program I was participating in at the time. One of the members of this group is a Chief Executive who has significant experience as a client working with consultants. In the course of our discussions two issues were raised which I did not consider in depth at the time, but which have wider relevance for both consultants and clients. The first was the matter of the contract entered into by client and consultant. This can be seen as a simple thing: the client hires the consultant because she needs extra resources or because she wants the consultant to solve a particular problem which the client is already clear about. This is not how I was seeing the contract though. I saw the contract as being perpetually under negotiation and in the next section I will explore this view of the contract. The second issue raised in my learning group was whether or not I should have taken the contract in the first place and I will explore the ethical issues related to this after first looking at the question of the contract.

Contracts

The first point about the contract is identifying what the two parties are contracting to do together. Schein (1999) describes three roles for the consultant: the expert providing expertise; the doctor providing diagnosis; and the process consultant, facilitating the client through a process where knowledge of the content of the client's work is of secondary importance. Under Schein's classification, the TCorp project would be described as process facilitation, where I am helping the client work through a process to improve the situation they are in.

Nolan (2001) summarizes Block (1981) as suggesting that as well as determining the role of the consultant it is important for the long term success of the consulting project for the consultant to surface resistance during the contracting process. He emphasizes the importance of the relationship between the client and consultant and advocates distinguishing between the task to be performed and the feelings about each other as a means of building this relationship. In other words, the contracting process is essentially a communicative process in which the consultant and a person or people from the client organization are working out what they want to do and how they will work together. Inevitably planning (in the form of thinking) and action are involved, usually seen as occurring sequentially in that order. So for a consultant there is the thinking in the form of a proposal, and for the consultant and the client there is the thinking expressed in the contract which sets out the consultant's role in the relationship. Then there is action in the form of implementing the project in accordance with the contract. This treats the participants in the relationship as passive followers of the contract. A particular way of thinking about ethics goes along with this, which is that ethical behavior is that which enacts the contract as written down. The problem with this view is that it is very rare for the contract to set out the project in terms sufficiently expansive to guide every dilemma or challenging situation that arises during the course of the project. In fact, a common form of industrial disruption is known as "work to rule" where workers do only what is written down in the contract or procedure manual and nothing else, thereby crippling the business. In my experience, the contract usually sits in the bottom drawer and is not referred to again unless the project gets into trouble or the relationship breaks down. How, therefore, are we to explain what happens during a consulting engagement, if it is not that thought comes before action and the consultant and client think about the contract and the consultant then enacts what is written down in the contract?

At this point I turn to the theory of complex responsive processes (Stacey, 2003) which does not separate thought from action. This theory draws on Mead (1934) who suggested that meaning in interaction is co-created through a process of gesture and response, where a gesture means words, actions, facial expressions and so on, and the response to the gesture creates the meaning of the gesture, at the same time as it is being generated by the gesture. So if I yell at you, you could take it as a warning and thank me, or as an insult and yell back at me. There is no intrinsic meaning held in the yell itself, and neither of us knows the meaning of it until you respond. This is not to deny that I have intention in yelling, but the meaning we make of it is not known until the response is given, and of course the response itself is also a gesture calling forth its own response. So, communication can be seen as a continuing process of making meaning of these gestures and responses. We are able to do this because humans physiologically have the capacity to take on the response being called forth in the other (Stacey, 2003). Because humans anticipate the response to their gestures, they modify their gestures according to the response they expect as well as the response they receive. This is very different from the idea of a sender such as a client with a message or a contract describing what they want the consultant to do and a consultant decoding the message to understand what the client has said: Mead is suggesting that there is no intrinsic "true" meaning locked in a message, that gesture and response cannot be separated, and that the response cannot be predicted from the gesture. Under Mead's explanation, the contracting process consists of the consultant and the client making ever-evolving meaning together through this gesture-response process. In this way, the experience of the client and consultant is jointly constructed in what is essentially a social act. This describes in a way close to my own experience how we jointly construct the engagement and contract together.

   As a consultant I have found that assignments invariably change during their course to the degree that I now recognize the engagement process as part of the consultation assignment itself. To summarize, I am arguing that the contract is being perpetually constructed mutually with the client during the contracting phase and indeed throughout the course of the assignment.

Ethics

Members of my learning group raised a second issue when they suggested I should not have taken on the contract at all, given my misgivings and the way I had developed what could be seen as an undisclosed intention to change the work. It was suggested that continuing could even be unethical. It was a shock to be challenged on my ethics and the immediate temptation was simply to justify what I did. How are consultants to think of the ethics of this type of situation? One way is to compare a decision with a universal standard or rule, for example that it is wrong for me not to discuss my disagreement and intention to continue negotiating changes in the way the sessions were to be delivered. This is similar to Kant's ethics of autonomous individuals with freedom to make choices who are acting ethically when they act in such a way that their actions could become universal laws for everyone to follow (Griffin, 2002). Griffin argues that the approach of comparing possible actions to a universal standard assumes that humans can

> Understand their own actions in terms of the goals they set themselves as autonomous individuals and the judgments they make as to the ethics of their actions. In making such judgments, they formulate hypothetical imperatives and test actions against them, so discovering the nature of universal categorical imperatives.
>
> (Griffin, 2002: 205)

This amounts to saying that the individuals are applying scientific method to discover the universal standards which govern ethical behavior. It is based on the assumption that humans first think, then act. First they think about their possible actions, comparing them against the universal laws, and then they act. Ethical behavior is that which is in harmony with the universal laws, and unethical behavior is that which breaks a universal law. Humans discover these universal laws by formulating hypothetical laws which they test their actions against, and through this experimental process they discover these universal laws, in much the same way as a scientist conducts experiments to test a hypothesis. However, as I mentioned earlier, splitting thinking and action does not reflect what we as humans actually do. We are always thinking and acting at the same time in processes of ongoing relationship in specific contingent situations. Between client and consultant, the contract and the relationships are always evolving together.

How then, can one think about ethics in a way that does not rely on thought before action? As Mowles mentions earlier in this volume, there are more choices than either accepting an assignment and undertaking the work as I think the client wants it while feeling very constrained, and not taking on the work at all. Another way of thinking about ethics as ongoing negotiation is required. Again I turn to the theory of complex responsive processes and Mead's argument that the individual and the environment mutually determine each other, in which case, "the moral interpretation of our experience must be found within the experience itself" (Griffin, 2002: 147). Mead argued against the notion of "ethical universals apart from and before action and against which conduct is to be judged as ethical or not" (ibid.: 182) because it would imply that the meaning of an action could be known in advance. As mentioned earlier, Mead believed that meaning is created socially through the process of gesture/response, rather than being determined in advance by an individual. Mead's interest in physiology led him to assert that humans have the bodily capacity to take the attitudes of others. This means that, as well as having the freedom to choose their next acts, humans can also know and therefore be responsible for their own conduct, even though they cannot know in advance the outcomes of their actions. Griffin (ibid.: 160) says "ethics, good conduct, is the social process of individual participants knowingly interacting with each other and having to account to each other in an on-going, ordinary, everyday way for the detail of what they do in their local situation in the living present". This is a very different idea from comparing actions to a universal standard.

The enquiry sparked by my learning set led me to see the situation at Tcorp in terms of this view of ethics arising in ongoing negotiation with the client. The client has asked Richard and me, the consultants, to facilitate sessions they have largely designed, and we have agreed. This seems simple enough. However, at the time it was more unknown and more complicated than this for a number of reasons. There were significant unknowns and it seemed to me that the process of exploring these would present the opportunity to resolve the aspects I was uncomfortable about. Richard had a strong existing relationship with the client and Mary's presence was reassuring as I knew I would be able to talk frankly with her and that she would be an avenue for influencing other people in TCorp. At this point, although I had not met the client, Richard and I were both uncomfortable with the idea that managers would be put through a highly programed event that, while providing an interesting high energy experience, would take time and attention away from discussion to make sense of the new ways of working, identifying and resolving issues, and planning for the move. The questions about laptops and car spaces also suggested there could well be more "cans of worms" beneath the surface which I did not yet know about. I was hoping to agree with the client that the sessions would become forums for discussions to explore and surface the issues of status, identity and politics surrounding the move and changing ways of working, in order to provide a means of explicitly informing decisions and action taken as a result.

These unknowns and areas of grayness are fairly typical of most times where I have been engaged to assist a client. Clients usually have a sense of the problem they face, and often have ideas about how to solve it. During the contracting process the nature of the problem can seem to shift and change so that what is actually undertaken can sometimes bear little resemblance to what was initially proposed. The consultant's actions themselves during the process of engaging with the client influence the situation as it unfolds.

My prior thinking about the ethics of the engagement process had developed through being involved in tender processes. There have been numerous times when my reaction to reading one of these tender documents, or having an initial conversation with the client has been "what they are proposing will not work in that form". This would usually be either because at that point I did not agree in detail with the client's diagnosis of the situation, or else the proposed solution did not seem to match up to the client's own diagnosis. In my early days of consulting I pondered on whether or not I should bid for a job where I did not agree with the approach that was planned. There were several things which made me decide I would not let my initial doubts alone deter me. First, for projects within my sphere of expertise I believed I would do a good job, if not a better job than most. In which case the client would have lost out on a bid from a qualified person, and I would have lost out as well. Second, I had a growing recognition that I could not know enough about these projects from the initial discussion or just from reading the tender document and then providing a written proposal in response. Additionally, the process of reading a written document and then writing a proposal in response does not at all match up with the way consulting projects are done. The consulting projects I have been involved with have always involved mainly face to face conversation and interaction, with maybe written artifacts produced during the course of the assignment. I have never once had a consulting assignment where writing has been the primary means of communication between the client and me. However, several of the engagement processes I have participated in have consisted mainly of written communication. Third, most projects change significantly during the course of doing the work, from what was initially proposed. Given these ever shifting sands of engaging with a client, a stance of only responding to consulting opportunities where I agreed with a clearly spelt out solution determined in advance was an unrealistic ethical standpoint if I wanted to earn a living through consulting.

Reflecting on the contracting process and associated ethics has highlighted for me the importance of ideology and the ethics arising in the process of the ongoing negotiation between client and consultant which takes place during contracting and throughout the course of an engagement. At the time we do not know what is going to happen next and what can seem very complex at the time can seem quite simple with the benefit of hindsight. To me, thinking of the ongoing process of negotiation better reflects the ethical situation in TCorp than the notions of universal standards, thought before action, or vision and values. The ethics of the situation arise in how we account to each other for what is going on between us. And this, I think, leads to what may be the biggest development in my thinking from undertaking the reflective process of writing this chapter in terms of what it means to consider ethics as arising in a process of ongoing interaction. I am starting to see the accountability we have to each other as a responsibility to keep discussing, to keep exploring and raising these differences in thinking.

The project was moving from the contracting stage into the work of the project itself and the next task was to design the sessions. I was looking forward to discussing with the client how the sessions would be designed and facilitated. At this point in the relationship I had not met the client personally and although I had discussed with Richard our differences in thinking, I did not feel the time was yet right to raise them directly with the client. This theme was to continue during the consulting assignment and had a material impact on how the project developed in ways I was not expecting.

Designing the sessions

Once we agreed to undertake the project with its reduced scope, Richard and I spent a morning together looking at the design of the sessions and planning how we thought we could make use of the public relations company's main design elements, while adjusting the way they were facilitated, so that there would be the opportunity for some less structured conversations. We prepared a rough outline of how we would conduct the sessions. That afternoon we went in to meet the client and talk through the sessions. The meeting was held at the public relations company's offices and was significant because this was the first time I was to meet the client.

The client's project people arrived on time, we were introduced to everybody and I had a warm reunion with Mary. I had not seen her for a couple of years. We assembled in the meeting room and the public relations company talked through their ideas for the sessions. It was a rather tricky meeting for me because I was meeting everybody, apart from Richard and Mary, for the first time. At this point, mainly because I lived in one city and everyone else in another, I had met neither the client nor the public relations company and had not discussed anything about the project directly with them; I had spoken with Richard who had then talked with the client. However, we both felt well prepared for the meeting. As the ideas for the sessions were revealed I knew I did not agree with the design ideas or the thinking behind them. At some stage Richard and I were going to have to comment and I did not feel I had struck a sufficient relationship for it to survive me being critical of the ideas. At the same time I felt concerned as I heard the ideas and knew I could not support what I was hearing. Richard and I exchanged several glances as the ideas for the sessions were displayed, culminating in the idea of having managers blindfolded and put into rowing boats where they were to row the boats with pieces of wood around a marker guided only by the verbal instructions of other team members. The client's people seemed to be considering the ideas and eventually asked Richard and me what we thought of what we had heard. Focusing on the rowing boat idea, I pointed out that we would not have time to do such an activity and that therefore we would need to come up with another idea that took less time and was more directly related to the task that managers would have to complete after the workshops, namely, identify potential problems and plan for their move. By now the climate in the room was polite but slightly tense and we suggested one or two alternative ideas which were turned down. Concluding that this meeting was not a good occasion to be suggesting design ideas or attempting to collaborate, we agreed that Richard and I would prepare a suggested plan and develop a draft session outline to review.

The whole group then went to another room where we viewed the first cut of the video that had been produced, showing the CEO speaking positively about the desired culture and also using a local comedy performer to give a light hearted perspective on the changes and the move. Everyone in the room seemed to enjoy the video immensely, yet I found myself uncomfortable with aspects of it, and was unclear as to whether this was because I had predetermined that I would not like any of the public relations company's work, or whether there was any real foundation in my dislike of the video. The video showed the comedian in "mockumentary" style interviewing people saying how much they liked being in their relevant category of being telephone-based, roaming and so on, parodying the approach seen in infomercials where satisfied customers give testimonials about how much they like the product. I knew one aspect of the planned use of the video I did not like was that it was intended to have a crackling static introduction which would just come on and interrupt the facilitator's introduction, and they wanted me to act as though I was surprised and pretend it was a live video feed from headquarters interrupting the session.

After the meeting had concluded, Richard and I discussed what had occurred. It was becoming clearer that the client wanted not a facilitator, but what I would call a master of ceremonies, someone to link together a series of pre-programed activities, rather than someone to pose questions and foster discussion about the changes. Neither of us was comfortable with this approach, even though we had been reassured on a number of occasions by the client that the organization's culture was such that the line managers liked and expected a "wow" factor and a highly polished programed production. We were still certain the session would be more useful if it incorporated opportunities for discussing the changes, and we still hoped to influence the client in this direction.

More on ethics

As I reflect on these events now, I am noticing my inability during the meeting either to find words to express more directly my concerns or to ask questions to explore the thinking behind the ideas being proposed. I felt safe pointing out that there would not be time for the rowing boats idea but not in pointing out that I did not think the rowing boats and other activities would help managers deal with the changes coming up. I was finding what I thought would be a less contentious side issue to give as a reason not to proceed with that idea. My awareness that I was at the beginning stage of developing a working relationship with those in the room loomed large and I thought that if I stated that I disagreed with the entire approach then I would never be able to establish a good working relationship with them. This pattern of me not expressing what I truly thought is a theme that continues throughout this assignment with this client and had the effect of covering over what I now see as an important aspect of the project – the client and I had different views of how the sessions should be designed in order to achieve the objectives set out in our contracting process.

Perhaps this may have been an opportunity for me to withdraw from the project, which raises the question of whether I should do this when there is already a contract in place. From a contractual point of view the ethical thing to do would be to continue to perform the agreed contract as planned. Withdrawing would amount to renegotiating the terms of the contract for early termination. If the contract is to be renegotiated for early termination then that suggests other terms could well be up for renegotiation as well. I note that the contract was silent on what would happen if there was a disagreement on how to carry out the assignment, but nevertheless this is confirming the ongoing negotiated processes involved in consulting assignments. As it happened, withdrawing did not occur to me at this stage because I was confident of being able to work these questions through with the client as the project went along. After all, in designing sessions there are usually many opportunities to review together the design and finalize the approach. But I was still very conscious of the signed contract and I would have felt I was leaving the client and Richard in the lurch without sufficient time to make alternative arrangements to replace me. In fact, I felt my task was to work together with the client to get the best results from these sessions and improve or add value on what they would have done without me.

In reflecting on these events now it has become important to me to try to understand how we were thinking differently and the impact this difference had on the subsequent development of our relationship and the consulting work. I think this is something consultants do not generally do; it is certainly something I have not generally done in my consulting life. The process of reflecting on this and writing this chapter has made me think more deeply about situations where projects develop in ways the consultant had not really expected. My inability to point out at the time the difference in our thinking had a direct result on the way this project developed and I think that reflecting on these differences in thinking and making them explicit with the client could improve both relationships and the consulting work. I am changing my view of what consulting is. I am starting to see consulting as participating in conversations that surface and discuss different ways of thinking, that explore the taken-for-granted assumptions about organizations and how it is we explain what we are doing together.

The thinking underlying the design of the sessions

A key to understanding what was going on was my feeling of discomfort with what was planned. This stemmed from my emerging awareness of the taken-for-granted assumptions behind this design and how my thinking was changing about the value of this type of session in organizational change. Conducting group sessions for managers is a key tactic in planned change, which has its roots in the response through the 1930s to 1960s to the increasing pace of change and the desire to understand methods of directing social change (Dewey, 1935). Immediately it is apparent that behind this brief statement of the intent of planned change is the assumption that social change can be controlled to achieve a certain desired result. This reflects the belief that thought occurs before action, and the notion of the designer of the change stepping outside of the system in order to plan what change other people, in the form of the system, need to make. Interestingly, planned change was initially seen as a kind of "middle ground" between on the one hand a "laissez faire" economic approach reflecting the view that tampering with the natural and social universe interferes with the homeostatic forces that if left to their own devices will produce a maximized outcome, and on the other hand, a Marxist emphasis on conflict, class struggle and radical intervention (Bennis *et al.*, 1969). Planned change is seen as self-consciously and experimentally employing social technology to help solve the problems of people and societies. Planned change attempts to apply scientific research to social and organizational problems in order to solve them and bring about desired results. It means engineering the workings of organizations to achieve a desired end.

Chin and Benne (1969) suggest that planned change strategies fall into three types. First, empirical/rational strategies assume that people are rational beings who follow their rational self-interest once this is revealed to them. These strategies involve proposing and presenting a change as being in the self-interest of those affected by the change. Second, the normative/re-educative group of strategies assume that patterns of action and practice are supported by people's commitment to socio-cultural norms, attitudes and value systems, and involve tactics aimed at changing normative orientations including values, skills and significant relationships. Power/coercive strategies are the third group and emphasize political and economic sanctions as well as moral power with its associated processes of guilt and shame. At TCorp the managers are seen as leverage points who will affect the success of the change. All three types of strategies had been incorporated into the design of this program; an example of an empirical/rational strategy being selling the change as being in the interests of participants, and an example of the normative/re-educative approach being increasing participants' commitment to the corporate values. There was also what those in TCorp called the "name and shame" process as an example of the third type. "Name and shame" was the apparently common process of the leader of the group naming one by one each individual who had not completed their task, or achieved whatever the target was. Each person in turn would stand and experience the shame of being named as one of those who were not doing their part.

It is clear that from this perspective, the organization is viewed as a whole made up of systems nested in systems, which are more or less in stable equilibrium. As a system it is composed of parts at different levels such as the individual, the team, the business unit and the organization. Each level of the system has a boundary between itself and its environment; equilibrium is seen as its natural state. The tendency to equilibrium is seen as a source of resistance to change and the system cannot change on its own, it requires an external force to cause it to change its state. Cause and effect are seen as closely linked in the sense that this program will cause managers to promote the change and the effect will be a smooth move. The designer of the change and managers of the system at each level have the role of stepping outside of the system of which they are a part, using rational thinking to work out a defined future state, and hence the type of system needed, as well as a series of planned actions to bring about the desired organizational end state. The system's parts together make up the whole and the whole is also ascribed causative power, referred to sometimes as culture, soul, or heart. The designer of the change plans out the steps to reach the end result. Stacey *et al.* (2000) refer to this as rationalist causality. Then the sessions are held and after the sessions, the system unfolds its purpose in accordance with the plan, with the help of additional management actions to solve problems, make further plans and so on which are also seen as necessary to overcome resistance to change and the organization's culture or history. As time goes by the organization is considered to be unfolding its potential, which has been unlocked by the leader or designer through the interventions they have initiated. Stacey *et al.* (2001) refer to this as formative causality, where the organization is unfolding the purpose already contained within it. The problem with organizational thinking based on rationalist and formative causality is that it ignores the contradiction of the designer or manager exerting rationalist cause in designing the system and then being themselves subject to formative cause inside the organization. Nor does it explain what causes the designer to design the system differently, or how the designer figures out what design or interventions are required. How are we to explain organizational change in a way that avoids the problem of (taken-for-granted) shifts between the two types of causality?

One way is to avoid thinking of the organization as a system in this taken-for-granted way. If an organization is not a system, then what is it? At the time of the project with TCorp, I had just about finished my first paper for the doctoral research program and so I was influenced by Stacey (2001) who suggests organizations are complex responsive processes of relating that do not form a whole or other level, rather they lead to patterns of further complex responsive processes of relating. Mead's gesture/response process of interaction which I referred to earlier is replicated throughout the organization. Drawing on Elias (1978), these interactions are characterized by power differentials which are a feature of all human relating, and which arise through differences in each party's relative need for each other. The parties cannot just do anything if they want to stay in relationship with each other, they are constrained in what they can do which creates patterns of similarity and consistency over time. At the same time, the potential for novelty is always present because the response of the others cannot be predicted. From these myriad interactions, widespread patterns of consistency and novelty emerge. By analogy from the complexity sciences, some of these small novelties are amplified into large effects in the patterns of interaction, but these cannot be predicted in advance.

There was a time when I was quite comfortable with the thinking behind planned change but my work on the doctoral program was changing the way I saw what we were doing at TCorp. The theory of complex responsive processes was still very new to me and I did not feel confident enough to bring this up in discussion with the client. What I am seeing now is that reflecting on these differences in our ways of thinking and making these differences explicit is the ethical challenge inherent in these interactions in which meaning is constantly being negotiated.

A public relations exercise

I have discussed above the approach to planned change and my nascent thinking from complex responsive processes in the process of contracting for the project and in designing the sessions. The public relations company's involvement was bringing an additional discourse to the mix, and this seems significant to me. They were being engaged to design a workshop to help people prepare for moving into a new building and to get them comfortable with the new ways of working. The move and new ways of working therefore were being seen as public relations issues. Is this signaling that the managers and staff of the organization were being treated as a public similar to external publics, and the techniques of organization development were being utilized as a way of adding power to a public relations exercise?

The origins of public relations: propaganda

Edward Bernays is regarded as the father of public relations. He prided himself on being a propagandist and came to early prominence as part of the US War Department's Committee on Public Information in 1918 when the term "propaganda" came into common language through the Allies equating the term with big black lies used by the Hun. The Committee on Public Information did a brilliant job of making the British and American publics believe that the Germans told lies while the Allies told facts, and they were able to generate mass enthusiasm about World War I. This was quite a feat because they were able to generate support for a global brawl that would otherwise have mystified those masses, and which actually killed and harmed, physically and psychologically, many of those very masses who supported it (Bernays, [1928] 2005). Public opinion was seen as a force to be managed by trained experts, a supra-governmental body of detached professionals, the "responsible administrator" of Lippmann ([1922] 1997), the "invisible governors" of Bernays (op. cit.) who coolly keep it all together from a distance. After the war Bernays applied his techniques on behalf of business clients. His approach was to identify the prevailing custom and work to change it so that his product would appear to recommend itself to people. For example, when he sold Mozart pianos he did not simply hype the pianos. He carefully sought to "develop public acceptance of the idea of a music room in the home" (Bernays, [1928] 2005: 78), to sell the pianos indirectly through making it seem essential to have the proper space in the home for a piano.

Bernays pioneered a number of features which are now commonly used in internal organizational communication. These include explaining his techniques as a set of rational steps to achieve a predetermined purpose, standing outside the organization and its publics to design the interactions between them, using survey feedback as part of analysis prior to intervention, and using a sponsoring committee or reference group.

Public relations techniques commonly used in organizational communication

Bernays describes a three staged approach to his campaigns. First, he would analyze the client's situation, then analyze the target audience or public before formulating policies governing the general practice, procedure and habits of the client (ibid.: 66). I was struck when I read this, by the similarity between this approach and my needs assessment (Rossett, 1987) approach as an instructional designer and consultant, both of which included analyzing the client's situation and the group of affected people, whether they were a group of people to be trained or a group of people being affected by change, prior to designing the solution, or in Bernays' words, "formulating the policy".

Bernays holds that a public relations counsel should anticipate the trends of public opinion and either convince the public that its fears or prejudices are unjustified or advise the client to modify actions to the extent necessary to remove the cause of the complaint. Here, he could be describing a typical organization development intervention: "public opinion might be surveyed and the points of irreducible opposition discovered" (Bernays, [1928] 2005: 95). Survey feedback from internal groups is a classic instrument in the OD armory and interventions are often based on the results of survey feedback (e.g. Miles *et al.*, 1969).

I was also somewhat surprised to find that the idea of the sponsoring committee or steering group, commonly used in project management methodology (e.g. Kerzner, 2003; Meredith and Mantel, 2003), had its genesis in Bernays' propaganda techniques. A steering group is a group of top level people with authority within the organization who meet regularly to approve the project and keep it on track. A reference group is a group of people taken from the target audience and used to validate the project team's approach. Bernays first began to use these ideas in 1913 when he pulled together an authoritative-seeming committee of doctors to provide medical credibility and approve the Broadway production of Eugene Brieux's play *Damaged Goods*, which dealt forthrightly with the topic of venereal disease (Bernay, op. cit.).

Mark Crispin Miller, in his introduction to Bernays' book *Propaganda* ([1928] 2005) says (italics original) "Bernays sold the *myth* of propaganda as a wholly rational endeavor, carried out methodically by careful experts skilled enough to lead 'public opinion'" (ibid.: 20). This comment has direct parallels with the theory of strategic choice where the strategist, as careful expert, whether instructional designer, OD practitioner, manager or CEO, starts out with a goal or vision, and then designs a set of rational steps which will lead to achieving that goal or vision. Interestingly, Bernays talks of the propagandist pulling the wires that control the public mind, so that the propagandized do whatever the propagandist wants them to do, exactly as they are told, and without them knowing it. This is another example of what Stacey *et al.* call "formative cause" (Stacey, *et al.*: 2000) where members of the publics are seen to be carrying out the design of an intervention which has been created by others, such as the CEO, the manager, the consultant, or in Bernays' case, the propagandist. This way of thinking takes no account of the human ability to choose and exercise will.

Miller, in his introduction to *Propaganda* makes a point about the relationship between the organization and the media, saying "corporate propaganda squelches inconvenient journalistic enterprise, so that early warnings fail to resonate, and growing ills receive no mass attention" (Bernays, [1928] 2005: 26). If we substitute the words "divergent opinions" for "journalistic enterprise" then the statement would apply equally to a modern day organization. Later he says, "Bernays' campaigns were ... intended to pre-empt all discussion, if not all conception" (ibid.) of alternative ways of thinking or doing business. TCorp's structured, highly designed sessions with no space for discussion, were intended to pre-empt any alternatives so that the managers would accept moving into cramped conditions and like the new identities prescribed for them.

Publicity

Publicity, an essential component of the public relations portfolio, also works this way as pointed out by Habermas, "Publicity work is aimed at strengthening the prestige of one's own position without making the matter on which a compromise is to be achieved itself a topic of *public discussion*" (Habermas, 1989: 26). As well as the obvious link to the earlier-mentioned ethical accountability to bring more into the realm of public discussion, rather than less, what is included in the public domain for discussion and what is not plays a large part in the patterns of consistency and novelty that emerge from the myriad interactions that take place across an organization. Choices not to bring issues into the public domain tend to foster consistency and support the status quo, while choices to bring issues up for discussion, while they can be risky, create opportunity for new patterns of interaction to arise.

Staging events has long played an important role in generating publicity. Boorstin (1992) says that staging special events is one of the most effective and frequently used methods in public relations to control the circumstances surrounding an organization's interactions with its publics. Special events are another public relations tool pioneered by Bernays where, instead of waiting for happenstance to bring the organization and its publics together, the publicist creates an event in which the situation proceeds in ways that favor the organization. For example, Bernays was asked by a hotel owner for ideas to enhance the hotel's prestige and so improve its business. Instead of suggesting the hotel improve its service or its facilities, Bernays staged a glittering event to honor the hotel's 30th anniversary and celebrate the prestigious service the hotel had offered. A committee of prominent people was formed to direct and support the event (Bernays, [1923] 2004). The photographs were published, the event was reported and the mission was accomplished.

This event is "somewhat – but not entirely – misleading" (Boorstin, 1992: 102). How was it misleading? The hotel would not have been able to stage a posh event unless it had been providing some services to the community. However, if the services had been all that valuable, then recourse to public relations may not have been necessary. Boorstin (1992) points out that once the celebration has been held, the celebration itself becomes evidence that the hotel really is a distinguished institution. The occasion actually gives the hotel the prestige to which it is pretending. The value of the celebration to the hotel owners depends on it being photographed and reported widely. Boorstin (1992: 33) calls this a "pseudo event" and identifies four characteristics of pseudo events which are:

- Not spontaneous. Someone has planned or incited the event.
- Planned primarily, but not necessarily exclusively for the purpose of being reported or reproduced.
- That its "realness" is less important than its newsworthiness and ability to gain favorable attention.
- Intended to be a self-fulfilling prophecy.

At TCorp, the event on the boat as conceived by the public relations firm certainly seems to meet these criteria. Every planned intervention would meet the first criterion above by definition. One could argue that the high energy approach, funny video, putting people into dinghies and so on, were intended to have "gossip power" and be reported on back at the office as memorable. The emphasis on high impact activities and presentations seemed to indicate that "realness" was less important than favorable attention. It was intended that the idealized world depicted in the video and activities would lead to this idealization being enacted at work, that it would become a self-fulfilling prophecy. Anybody who has attended a high powered sales conference or multi-level marketing convention will know how an ideal world of dedication, hard work and success can be portrayed with such excitement and intensity that participants move to a heightened state of suggestibility.

These states of heightened suggestibility occur when normal physiological brain states are accidentally or deliberately disturbed through fear, anger or excitement, and they can give rise to temporarily impaired judgment (Sargant, 1997). In other words, when one's physiology is altered, either accidentally or deliberately, one can become more suggestible, to the extent that one's beliefs can change. Common ways of generating these states include chanting, drumming or rhythm, large group activities generating excitement (for example, multi-level marketing conventions, or large group awareness training), lack of sleep, shame and humiliation, and long periods of uncertainty. Prolonging the uncertainty and unknown elements are one way of making people more amenable to suggestion. The "hot desking" concept as used by TCorp creates uncertainty for the employees who arrive at work each day and have to find a spare desk to sit at. "Will the desk I like be taken? Will I have to sit next to someone I do not get on with?" These questions raise employees' levels of anxiety and suggestibility. The "name and shame" process of subjecting individuals to public confessions of their sins and subsequent humiliation is another practice of heightened suggestibility.

TCorp placed a significant emphasis on its image with its customers and other publics as a "funky" brand. Careful attention to public relations, marketing and spin is a strong aspect of the way the organization operates. There is an increasingly stronger awareness of the emphasis on public relations in wider society. For example, the spin doctors, with their ability to elevate appearance above substance are now considered de rigueur in election campaigns.

Summary of the argument so far

I have shown similarities between techniques commonly used internally in organizations today and techniques such as survey feedback and steering groups pioneered by Edward Bernays in the early days of public relations. I have also drawn a parallel between the use of highly designed group experiences used internally, and Boorstin's concept of the pseudo event, which is an event that has been created with the primary purpose of being reported in order to gain favorable attention. Through these sessions designed to have high impact on participants, the company is treating the staff as another constituency similar to their customers, politicians, shareholders and other stakeholders, using the same public relations techniques with respect to the staff as they would in relation to customers or politicians they must lobby. The sessions are designed to focus attention on some aspects of what is going on, for example the new identities represented by the new categories of working, and at the same time distract attention from other aspects, for example, that the space is smaller. This is very similar to how public relations activities will focus on information beneficial to the organization and distract attention away from aspects that are not favorable to the organization. One major difference is that with public relations, people are more aware that this is going on. With the planned change intervention, the managers and staff are far less aware of the dynamics of highlighting favorable aspects and downplaying less favorable aspects. These are the unacknowledged motives behind the design of the intervention.

I am also suggesting that these sessions represent an example of a blurring of the lines between public relations and organization development as this is not an isolated example. The public relations industry is aware of this as an important development in the industry. At the 2005 Annual General Meeting of the Chartered Institute of Public Relations, Judith Phair, who is Chief Executive of the Public Relations Society of America (PRSA) said "We're getting competition from management consultants, lawyers, and accountants who may portray us as strictly tacticians – only media relations. In fact, a PRSA Counselor's Academy survey last year ranked this as one of the most important challenges to the profession" (Phair, 2005). The public relations industry is aware of the loosening of its boundaries with other professions. The challenge for organization development practitioners will be to understand their own motivations and the motivations of others involved in their initiatives, as well as the thinking behind public relations practice in order to participate in conversations where these motivations are made discussable.

As a result of my lack of awareness of these motivations in the project with TCorp, I found myself increasingly unable to influence the direction of the project. By not being able to find a way to discuss these unacknowledged motives, I ended up attempting to influence the project through manipulation, while myself being pressured to collude with a public relations exercise. I became caught up in a process that seemed harder and harder for all of us – the client and the public relations people as well as me – to find a way forward together that we were happy with.

Facilitating the sessions

In subsequent discussions, Richard and I agreed with the client and public relations people on a revised plan for the sessions that we believed we could work with. In the meantime, Mary, my friend I was relying on to help me influence the project, had left. Although I did not know why, I suspected that personal differences played a part. The public relations people had selected a boat as the venue for the sessions, which were being run in the afternoon from 1 pm to 5 pm. I arrived in the morning of the first session in plenty of time to locate the boat and get set up. Richard had checked the boat and although he said it was small he thought it would be workable. When I found the boat being maneuvered into place a feeling of alarm kicked me in my stomach as I realized it was far too small, particularly for the first pilot group of 20 people. There was not enough room for participants to sit in a circle and so we had to do theater style seating, but that was not the only limitation of the boat, and I wished I had been more involved in selecting the venue. The large video screen was in a small room at the front of the boat, and the only room large enough to take all the participants had a tiny video screen. The latter room had walls of tarpaulins flapping in the wind and so flip charts could not be stuck to them. There was not sufficient space on the boat for the magnet boards and posters the public relations people had prepared. There was, to my mind, a whole catalog of shortcomings.

During the day, which I facilitated as best I could, one major disadvantage with the theater seating was that it was hard to get discussion going. The project manager, Sinead, was very nervous. During the day at every possible break opportunity, she anxiously came up to me with suggestions for how to do the job better. In truth, it reminded me of myself in earlier days when I organized my first training sessions for senior managers and how I had behaved similarly toward the facilitators I had engaged.

She was very concerned about the participants' energy levels, and keeping the sessions "strategic", not wanting to go into detail because at a later stage she had planned communications which would cover the details of the move. Therefore, she did not want these details discussed during this session. Sinead was the only one who knew answers to the questions, and unfortunately participants were asking these questions now, in advance of when it was planned that they would need to know the answers; questions such as where would they park their cars, what sort of desks would they have and would there be fridge space for their lunches. Reluctantly I told them it was planned to answer these questions at a later stage of the project. As it happened, I felt somewhat vindicated when, during the feedback session with participants at the end, they pointed out that it appeared we were avoiding the questions on their minds, and recommended we provide time for these questions and make sure we answered them.

When the pilot session was over I sat down with the project team for a debrief that took two and a half hours. I came away from it with a list of things to do differently. Although Sinead did not say so directly, I sensed she was unhappy with the way the day had gone, and that she did not think I had facilitated the day the way she wanted. I understood her to be saying that I was not energetic enough, and that if I only had more energy and did things the way she wanted them done, the session would go much better. She still wanted me to keep the sessions "strategic" and not allow the group to go into detail. We agreed to meet the next day at the venue at 11am to get the boat set up for our 1pm start. That night my mind was extremely active and I spent some time determining how I would handle the session with the General Managers the next day.

I was at the venue at around 10am, but by 12 o'clock no one else had arrived, so I was becoming concerned about getting the boat set up. I had done what I could but others had additional equipment and the key to get into the cabin proper. At 12.30pm Sinead arrived with yet other new people and a number of copies of the original creative brief from the public relations company. She asked me to come inside and dialed the public relations company's account manager for an audio conference during which they went through a large number of changes they had decided to make to the program that I was about to facilitate. My reactions were numerous and varied. First, shock, horror and amazement that this situation could be happening – that the client could be an hour and a half late and then tell me about the changes they had unilaterally made, only 30 minutes prior to the session beginning. There had clearly been a meeting about the session in which I had not been included. My confidence drained away like bathwater. I was furiously angry, wanting to stop listening to what they were saying and march off in a fit of pique. I was not sure I could change the running order so drastically with so little notice and still maintain a sense of flow. I was resentful and did not want to change what I had planned to do. It was one of those situations where I went into survival mode, just trying to stay alive there. I listened as much as I could, even though I so strongly wanted to angrily run away. I even summarized my understanding of what they wanted – feeling proud of myself as I did so. When they agreed that I understood what they were asking for, I explained I needed some time on my own to process and withdrew quietly by myself.

During my "time out", I resolved to continue with facilitating the session and go out there and perform the best I could, because of the contract we had, and the lack of time for them to find a replacement. It was perhaps the most difficult situation of my consulting career so far. I was very unsure what to do. I tried to imagine how two of my friends whose facilitation skills I admired would handle the client and tried to emulate what I thought they might do. In the end I got through the session and was pleased with the job I did because there were two turning points during the session. One was when the General Managers admitted they could not see the benefits to them of hot desking, and so they did not feel they could confidently discuss this with their people. The second was the realization they had relied on the hype and excitement of the move to make sure the move would go smoothly and that not everyone would necessarily be feeling as excited about it as they had assumed. To me these insights were evidence of achieving the purpose of the session.

After the session finished, Sinead's boss came down to the boat and we sat down for another blow by blow debrief taking one and a quarter hours. She clearly did not agree that these insights had been important for the participants, and it seemed we were seeing the situation quite differently from each other. I felt much criticized, as though my facilitation skills were under extreme scrutiny with little or no acknowledgment of the trying conditions and what we had managed to achieve. My attempts at pointing this out to a client who did not agree sounded like self-aggrandizement. There was so much I wanted to say but in the moment I could not find the words, or even a place to start. We seemed to be stuck in a position from which there was no way out. All the while during these interactions the tension was rising, as indeed it had been all day. Sinead had appeared anxious and worried all day and I thought she was concerned that it would all go wrong if it was not done the way she wanted, and I was concerned that it would all go all wrong if it was not done the way I wanted.

How did it arise that we became stuck so that there seemed to be no way out? Looking back I see that we were both unaware of how we were trying to control the situation and the reason we could not extract ourselves was because it remained undiscussable. I am now noticing how I did not express what I was thinking or feeling. The collusive process was that I was trying to deliver what they were asking for, on the one hand, but I was also trying to change it on the other hand. I also see that, while the client's people had held their own meetings to redesign the program that morning without including me, I also had gone through a process of redesigning the session the previous night without involving the client. I felt locked into a conflict with the others in the project where either my ideas were right or theirs were. As I look back, I see the interaction as having involved them telling me what they wanted, and me responding to that by trying to look like I was doing what they wanted, while at the same time figuring out ways to do what I thought was needed.

All of this was the consequence of the interplay of our various intentions to stay in control. The client did not want the car spaces and laptop status issues discussed because of the fear that this could lead to discussion or behavior that they would be unable to control. I was worried that if I directly opposed my client then they would react in a way I could not control and this might affect my reputation in the future. It seems significant to me that the levels of emotional tension were very high because they were telling me what I had done wrong even though I was not agreeing that I had done it wrong. It may have been helpful at the time to draw attention to the process we were involved in, but I did not. High levels of emotion are not usually referred to in the consulting literature, where the consultant is seen as a detached third party providing expert advice and support. But I believe they play a part that is under-recognized. There is an aspect in which I think facilitating a group is like a performance, full of risk. There is fear and anxiety for both facilitator and participants. Often at the end of such a session that has gone well, I feel a sense of satisfaction, fulfillment and sometimes even exhilaration. In fact that feeling of exhilaration is one of the things I love about this type of work.

During this discussion the power differentials between the client and me were being accentuated and shifting toward the client. They were telling me what I should do, and how I should do it, and in the process their power as the client was increasing. My concern about having a client who was not happy with my work and my concern about my reputation and how to handle the situation were all contributing to me feeling the power balance was being tilted away from me. I am not saying that power is something one party has over another, and that the client had power over me. What I am pointing to is the shifting dynamic of the power balance in our interdependence, (Elias, 1978) because this was where I started to lose confidence in my ability to move this consulting assignment to a conclusion we would all be happy with. As I lost confidence, so I lost power and felt helpless to raise for discussion the process we were caught in. I am seeing the fact that the process, motives and power dynamics remained undiscussable as the key ethical issue involved in this situation.

The end of the assignment

I discussed what had happened with Richard that night. The next day, he met Sinead and her boss, who told him they were unhappy with the program and were going to get one of their internal people to redesign the sessions, and that

Sinead would co-facilitate with us. Richard's response was to suggest that maybe they did not need the help of external facilitators any longer, which they agreed with, but said they wanted to give us the chance to continue because of the existence of the contract. After further discussion, the outcome was that Richard and Sinead took the opportunity to terminate the contract at this point.

What is facilitation?

Although both the client and I were describing my role during the sessions as "facilitation", the key to the conflict between us was that we both had quite different ways of understanding the nature of facilitation, and these differences were not discussed between us. Sinead at this stage did not want the group to explore how it would solve problems and make decisions related to the move. She was judging the sessions' effectiveness by the degree to which they got the group participants to accept the changes with a minimum of resistance, meaning a minimum of questioning or challenge to the plans. It now seemed that she desired a high energy, entertaining "master of ceremonies" to introduce the various stages of the session, link together the prepared experiences, and promote and sell the move and new ways of working to the participants. I am thinking of a sparkling infomercial television front person or presenter who narrates the story, links the segments, and acts as the enthusiastic voice of the program. This is a role that I imagine a public relations company would be very familiar with.

My own conception of facilitation has been influenced by instructional design and organization development, and more recently by the theory of complex responsive processes. The origins of the word "facilitate" include the concept of making something easy or more convenient (Hunter *et al.*, 1994), and so for me facilitation has always had a sense of helping a group to make progress. As a designer and facilitator of individual learning my role was to provide conceptual models, demonstrate how to perform activities and provide opportunities for practice (Mager and Pipe, 1984). Over time I became more involved in group sessions where my job was not to teach people how to do something, but rather to help them solve problems or undertake strategic planning. Schwarz was an influence in my evolution from facilitator as teacher, and he says:

> Group facilitation is a process in which a person who is acceptable to all members of the group, substantively neutral, and has no decision-making authority intervenes to help a group improve the way it identifies and solves problems and makes decisions, in order to increase the group's effectiveness.
>
> (Schwarz, 1994: 4)

In terms of meeting these criteria, I had been selected through a formal process as being an acceptable facilitator, and I certainly had no decision-making authority. Although in both Schwarz's conceptualization and the client's, I was not expected to hold views of my own, both the client and I differed from Schwarz in that neither of us expected me to be substantively neutral, however our expectations in this regard were different. The client expected me to be an enthusiastic advocate, promoting and selling the move and the new ways of working to the group. I expected to be discussing with them their views of the move and to be helping them to plan for the move, solving problems and making decisions along the way. This was a key way of thinking that I did not discuss with the client, and if I had it may have made all the difference.

Schwarz's definition of facilitation is aligned with Schein's process consulting idea of the neutral consultant who distinguishes between content and process. This is certainly a distinction that has informed my thinking about facilitation, but is not a natural or easy thing to do in the natural ebb and flow of conversation, as Schein points out:

> One of the toughest tasks for the consultant/helper is not to get seduced by the content, not to get so caught up in the actual problem the group is working on as to cease to pay attention to *how* it is working.
>
> (Schein, 1999: 150)

My views of what facilitation is have been shifted though, through my work on the Doctor of Management program, in particular reading Shaw (2002), who suggests that not only is the process/content distinction encouraging facilitators to think about the group process or patterning in human relating that emerges over time, a process that is not the intention of any single individual or group; it also posits "that people can introduce new patterns that they do intend" (ibid.: 9). She says that this has encouraged facilitators, consultants and managers informed from this tradition, and I include myself in this, to "work as if they must propose well-designed patterns for all interaction in advance of interacting, as though that is what being enabling entails" (ibid.: 9–10). The need for process facilitation to keep things on track occurs, she says, because in spite of the intentions of the designer to produce the best session design, to introduce the new desired, planned patterns of relating, unwanted patterns of conversation will continue to arise.

Another of Shaw's insights that was helpful to me was how working out in advance things like the outcomes, procedures for working together, prepared presentations, all reduce the experience of uncertainty. She says that "the experience of acting into the known is engineered – participants know what they should do and know what the outcome should be" (ibid.: 32). All this engineering of the experience increases the likelihood of "people constructing the familiar together" (ibid.: 32). In other words, it works toward keeping things the same, rather than working toward changing the way people work together. This struck me strongly. Designing the session in advance and seeing facilitation as carrying out the design of the session actually works against the desired outcomes.

I was seeing the purpose of the sessions as to provide a forum for the managers to make sense of what the changes meant and plan what actions they needed to take to insure the move went smoothly for their own teams. This meant I saw myself as encouraging discussion amongst the members of the group relating to various aspects of the changes so they could make their own sense of what was going to happen. This was not at all how the client was seeing it and the more they critiqued the day, the less confident I became. I did not have, in the moment, the ability to shift the conversation, or explain my view. Contributing to this was the undiscussability of our different ways of seeing the engagement and work of facilitation.

Conclusion

I am arguing that an organization is not a thing that the people in the organization can step outside of to diagnose and then step back inside of to enact a solution. Neither is a client's problem a thing they can step outside of, diagnose and then step back inside of to enact a solution. The very act of contracting with a consultant changes the situation in subtle and unpredictable ways. The process of contracting for a consulting engagement is not simply a matter of the client telling the consultant what they want and the consultant doing it. It is a jointly conducted negotiation during which the consultant and client together make meaning of the ever-evolving situation. The client and consultant cannot step outside the situation and so an ethics is required that locates the moral interpretation of the situation within the experience itself. Griffin (2002) suggests this is a process of accounting to each other for what we do. I am coming to see this accountability for effective consulting as including a well developed capacity for making discussable the taken-for-granted assumptions and ways of thinking operating in everyday situations.

Organization development and public relations both seek to apply scientific thinking to social situations, in organization development's case within the organization and in the case of public relations, outside the organization. There are a number of similarities between the techniques involved, such as survey feedback and steering groups. As organizations are increasingly using public relations companies for internal change work it seems that the boundaries of these two disciplines are blurring, to the degree that the public relations profession is seeing management consultants as an increasing source of competition. Companies are treating staff as another constituency similar to the way they see external publics. Organization development practitioners and consultants will have to be aware of this blurring of boundaries in order to avoid their work unwittingly becoming caught up in the execution of public relations exercises.

The distinction between process and content is widespread in the field of organization development and leads facilitators to design processes for others to follow, independent of the content. I am in agreement with Shaw (2002) that human relating is a process that takes place over time and is not in the control of any one individual, whether they be participant, facilitator, leader or manager. I also think that the concept of the detached facilitator keeping the process of human interaction on track hides the anxiety-filled emotional and exciting experience of acting into the unknown that I have found my consulting career to be.

References

Bennis, W. G., Benne, K. D. and Chin, R. (1969) *The Planning of Change (2nd Edition)*, New York: Holt, Rinehart and Winston.
Bernays, E. ([1923] 2004) *Crystallizing Public Opinion*, New York: Kessinger Publishing.
Bernays, E. ([1928] 2005) *Propaganda*, New York: Ig Publishing.
Boorstin, D. (1992) *The Image: A Guide to Pseudo-Events in America*, New York: First Vintage Books.
Chin, R. and Benne, K. D. (1969) "General strategies for effecting changes in human systems", in Bennis, W. G., Benne, K. D. and Chin, R. (eds.) *The Planning of Change (2nd Edition)*, New York: Holt, Rinehart and Winston.
Dewey, J. (1935) *Liberalism and Social Action*, New York: G.P. Putnam's Sons.
Elias, N. (1978) *What is Sociology?*, London: Hutchinson.
Griffin, D. (2002) *The Emergence of Leadership: Linking Self-Organization and Ethics*, London: Routledge.
Habermas, J. (1989) *The Structural Transformation of the Public Sphere*, Cambridge, MA: MIT Press.
Hunter, D., Bailey, A. and Taylor, B. (1994) *The Art of Facilitation*, Auckland, New Zealand: Tandem Press.
Kerzner, H. (2003) *Project Management: A Systems Approach to Planning, Scheduling and Controlling*, New Jersey: John Wiley & Sons.
Lippmann, W. ([1922], 1997) *Public Opinion*, New York: Free Press.
Mager, R. and Pipe, P. (1984) *Analyzing Performance Problems*, California: Lake Publishing.
Mead, G. H. (1934) *Mind, Self and Society: From the Standpoint of a Social Behaviorist*, Chicago: Chicago University Press.
Meredith, R and Mantel, S. (2003) *Project Management: A Managerial Approach*, New Jersey: J. Wiley.
Miles, M. B., Hornstein, H. A., Callahan, D. M., Calder, P. H. and Schiavo, R. S. (1969) "The consequence of survey feedback: Theory and evaluation", in Bennis, W. G., Benne, K. D. and Chin, R. (eds.) *The Planning of Change (2nd Edition)*, New York: Holt, Rinehart and Winston.
Nolan, M. (2001) "Stuckness and change in a community of organization consultants: my practice isn't my own", Unpublished thesis: University of Hertfordshire.
Phair, J. (2005) "Challenges facing the public relations industry", address to the Annual General Meeting of the Chartered Institute of Public Relations: London.
Rossett, A. (1987) *Training Needs Assessment*, California: Educational Technology Publications.
Sargant, W. (1997) *Battle for the Mind: A Physiology of Conversion and Brain-Washing*, Cambridge, MA: Malor.
Schein, E. H. (1999) *Process Consultation Revisited: Building the Helping Relationship*, Cambridge, MA: Addison-Wesley
Schwarz, R. M. (1994) *The Skilled Facilitator*, San Francisco: Jossey-Bass.
Shaw, P. (2002) *Changing Conversations in Organizations: A Complexity Approach to Change*, London: Routledge.

Stacey, R. D., Griffin, D. and Shaw, P. (2000) *Complexity and Management: Fad or Radical Challenge to Systems Thinking?*, London: Routledge.

Stacey, R. D. (2003) *Strategic Management and Organizational Dynamics (4th Edition)*, Essex: Pearson Education.

Stacey, R. D. (2005) "Organizational identity: The paradox of continuity and potential transformation at the same time", 29th S. H. Foulkes Annual Lecture to the Group Analytic Society: London.

Stacey, R. (2001) *Complex Responsive Processes in Organizations: Learning and Knowledge Creation*, London: Routledge.

Weick, K. (1995) *Sensemaking in Organizations*, Thousand Oaks, CA: Sage.

Index